"I finally found the book I woul
professor!), every pastor (and dei
leadership board (and committee)
Cameron Trimble is already respecteu as one of our top church consultants
and interdenominational networkers, but with *Piloting Church,* she also
distinguishes herself as one of our best religious writers. I feel like I just ate
a delicious meal including a perfect appetizer, fantastic main course, and
amazing dessert. Highly recommended!"
— Brian D. McLaren, author of *Cory and the Seventh Story*

"A gem of a book! Both philosophical and practical. Cameron Trimble
offers both nuggets of wisdom and practical steps for advancing beyond
stuck places. This book is for pastors, for sure, but it is really for anyone
who wants to be part of creating new spaces for the thriving of all creation."
— Alice Hunt, executive director, American Academy of Religion

"Cameron Trimble is an entrepreneurial and spiritual practitioner
extraordinaire. She dreams bigger than anyone I know, but has the skill
sets, the courage, the tenacity, and the talent to turn dreams into reality.
Piloting Church is her gift to leaders who want their own dreams for their
churches to come true. Filled with the practical, tactical, and strategic
genius she is known for, it is a beautiful combination of good theory and
sound advice, of dreaming big and working hard. If you want to lead with
vision and precision, put this book on your reading list and get ready to fly."
— John C. Dorhauer, general minister and president,
   United Church of Christ

"Our congregants are being detained by ICE. God's creation is threatened
by human-made climate change. LGBTQ people are denied their human
dignity. Trimble's book offers a flight plan for those willing to think and
lead communities to creatively and boldly live out the biblical call to
justice and love of neighbor."
— Jennifer Butler, CEO, Faith in Public Life

"In *Piloting Church,* Cameron Trimble gives us all the tools we need to
flourish in our ministries. Because of her abundance of experience working
with congregations in different denominations and settings, Rev. Trimble
can see the horizon clearly. If you are in church leadership, you should buy
this book, use this book, and get ready to take off!"
— Carol Howard Merritt, author of *Healing Spiritual Wounds* and
   I Am Mary

"If you care about your congregation's potential, Cameron Trimble is both an inspirational visionary and an incomparable practical guide. *Piloting Church* provides pastors and church leaders with the wisdom, insight, and motivation they need to fulfill the call and opportunity God is offering. A must read!"
— Jim Antal, United Church of Christ leader, climate activist, author,
    and public theologian

"A gem of a book, written out of passion for leaders who want to change the world propelled by the power of the Gospel. Through the lenses of a pilot, church and community leaders can take a fresh look at their strategic role in promoting health and vitality in churches embracing and serving their diverse contexts. Hurray for uncle James who encouraged Cameron to fly and discover new horizons, a similar dynamic found in Mordecai and Esther in the Old Testament. I wholeheartedly endorse this book because Cameron's witness and wisdom is much needed for 'such a time as this.'"
— Ruben Duran, director for congregational vitality,
    Evangelical Lutheran Church in America

"When it comes to church leadership in this season of our religious lives we faith leaders find ourselves flying blind. There's so much we can't see, and our human existence has never been messier. Many of us are holding space and leading organizations in a time in which our people are anxious, fearful of the future, worried about survival on every level, and longing for human and spiritual connection. In *Piloting Church* Cameron offers us the extraordinary gift of a flight plan. Not a recipe or an easy formula that promises a perfect outcome but a plan for the journey. Cameron's wisdom and instruction invite us to embody the qualities of an adaptive, creative, and visionary leader. She encourages us to trust ourselves, rely on the God who claims us, and dig deep to discover the courage to soar!"
— Shawna Bowman, pastor of Friendship Presbyterian Church, Chicago

PILOTING CHURCH

Helping Your Congregation Take Flight

CAMERON TRIMBLE

chalice
press

Saint Louis, Missouri

An imprint of Christian Board of Publication

ChalicePress.com

Print: 9780827231696
EPUB: 9780827231702
EPDF: 9780827231719

Printed in the United States of America

Contents

To Ann, who always knew I would fly

and

*to the team at the Center for Progressive Renewal, past and present,
who said yes to the adventure of "building the plane while flying it."*

Preface

This book is a combination of two great passions: leadership and flying. I was lucky enough to grow up with an uncle, James V. Corr, who was a fighter pilot in World War II. When he left the military for a career in the business world, he purchased a small single-engine Bonanza plane. It was in this plane that my love of flying was born.

Some of my earliest memories are of us climbing into the cockpit of the plane, careful to step only on the parts of the wing that could handle our weight as we slid into place. My uncle would go in first, situating himself in the pilot's seat. I would follow in the copilot seat, strapping myself in and readying myself for flight. His particular plane didn't have air conditioning and, in the Atlanta summer heat, the best we could do was open a tiny window in the side windshield and pray for a gust of air and a quick take off.

We would call to the tower: "Peachtree Ground, this is 711 Golf Sierra, at the Clairemont ramp, VFR to the northeast, with information Tango." We would wait to hear their response: "Roger 711 Golf Sierra, taxi via Bravo and Alpha to runway 3L for takeoff." Off we would go.

Few experiences prepare you for the first time you pull to the end of the runway. First, you line up on the centerline and then push the throttle forward. Slowly, your speed accelerates until you find your body pressed back against the seat and your eyes glued to the runway ahead. You watch your speed—45 knots, 50 knots, 55 knots—and then, suddenly, *it* happens: the beautiful combination of airspeed and wing angle create the lift you need to soar into the sky. It's like magic.

To this day, when I board massive 777 jumbo jets and fly across the country, I marvel at the science and art that is air flight. How can something so massive and so heavy fly seemingly effortlessly through the air, carrying us safely from one part of the world to another? I understand the four fundamentals of flight—thrust, drag, gravity and lift—and still I am in awe.

Leadership, when done well, creates the same sense of awe. Leadership is a unique art that comes from a careful balance of native instinct, self-discipline, and learned skills. When a church, organization, or team is led well, it can soar.

I have benefited from opportunities to step into a number of executive leadership roles very early in my life. I don't pretend to have this figured out, but I am learning that my two great passions—leadership and flying—have shared lessons that have strengthened my contribution to and engagement in both areas.

To date, I have cofounded and led five churches, businesses, or nonprofits. So far, all but one has been successful in meeting their missional and financial goals. While I still continue to lead some of these efforts, I am also finding much of my time is spent coaching others as they begin or further invest in their own endeavors. Most of my clients are pastors, nonprofit leaders, or denominational executives, all of whom are asking adaptive questions about the changes they need to lead their congregations or constituents through in this fast-paced, globally connected, ever-changing world.

My clients are very smart people, with a variety of backgrounds, who dream of making a positive difference in communities all across the country. They increasingly recognize that something significant is at stake in their work. All of them acknowledge that the work they are doing in their communities and on the national scale can either lead to a more just, generous, and peaceful world, or can end up a missed opportunity to help in this moment of great human transformation.

That is why I'm writing this book.

Right now, we need a real conversation about what effective leaders can do to create environments and systems that lead to human transformation. One of my favorite modern philosophers, a woman named Jean Houston, said in a presentation I attended some years ago, "The great challenge of our age is that we have developed the capacity to destroy ourselves without the wisdom to know not to do so." Today, our world faces crises on an unprecedented scale. We are destroying our planet through an endless consumerist culture that, as it turns out, is also killing our souls. We have developed our weapons of war to the level that we can destroy our world with the touch of a button. Global wealth distribution is creating a new class of the "haves" and the "have-nots" unprecedented in our country's history. Our community infrastructures—schools, hospitals, citizen groups, faith communities—are struggling to survive decreases in funding while also losing participation because, in part, we are all working 60+ hours a week to make ends meet. We are living in unsustainable ways, running on the treadmill of an unsustainable system, consuming our beautiful planet at unsustainable and unjust rates.

If ever there was a moment for a new cultural vision spoken and modeled by a new generation of leaders, this is that moment. May you be such a leader.

Henry Ford is quoted as saying, "Whether you believe you can do a thing or not, you are right."[1] I am on a mission to convince you that *your* leadership can make a difference in bold and great ways. After all, greatness is not something out of reach that only a few will ever attain. Greatness comes when you do what you love and do it greatly.

It is time to fly!

---

[1] See https://www.faa.gov/data_research/aviation_data_statistics/civil_airmen_statistics.

Chapter One

Decide You Want to Fly

Checklist

- ❐ Talk to people who are pilots; you should know what you are getting into

- ❐ Accept that your leadership matters...and will come at a cost and great joy

- ❐ Show up every day, without fail, ready to engage

- ❐ Give it everything you've got

- ❐ Don't get too committed to the outcome

"Courage does not consist of the absence of fear. Courage, rather, is the mastering of that fear: feeling the fear and going forward anyway."
—*Carey D. Lohrenz,*
U.S. Navy's First Female F-14 Tomcat Fighter Pilot

I knew from the time I was a little girl that I wanted to be a pilot. Sitting in the copilot seat of my uncle's Beechcraft Bonanza, far too short to see over the instrument panel, I studied the gas pressure gauges and tracked our flight on the old paper maps. We had a stopwatch taped to the pilot yoke and tracked our flight legs based on estimated times that we should arrive at each point. It was magic for me! Between those experiences and a few viewings of the "infamous" movie *Top Gun,* I knew that I was called to the skies.

I also knew that I wanted to make the world a better place. A few months ago, I stumbled upon a picture of my childhood bedroom. Most teenagers would have posters plastering their bedroom walls of the latest popular band or teen heartthrob. I had pictures of starving children in the African Sahara Desert and polluted rivers killing massive populations of fish in China. From a young age, I was concerned about the ways the world was broken. I wanted to dedicate what energy I could to make it all a bit better. So, in addition to being a pilot, I also knew that I wanted to be a pastor, believing the church was a great pathway to make the change in the world that I wanted to see. But as it is for many people, knowing what I wanted to do and figuring out a way to do it were two very different things.

The first challenge I faced as a young woman was that I didn't know any women who were pilots. Today, sadly, women still only make up 5 percent of the general aviation community. That means that out of all 454,000 licensed pilots in the United States, only 23,000 are women.[1] We've seen only a slight increase in the number of female pilots in the past 30 years. While I was told as a child that I could be anything that I wanted to be, I now recognize that because my imagination was limited by what I was seeing (or *not* seeing) in my world, I never seriously considered becoming a professional pilot. That changed for me, *slowly,* after I spent years on the road traveling on planes to and from conferences. I would see female pilots in the airport and something buried deep within would jolt to life, like a literal shock to my body. One day I was walking through the terminal in Hartsfield-Jackson International Airport in Atlanta, and I remember seeing a female pilot and thinking, "I know you. I recognize what drives you because it drives me too. You are most alive when you are in the air." The minute I found the courage to say that to myself, I didn't care that only a handful of women become pilots. I knew I was going to become one more.

Flying has taught me more lessons about life and leadership than I could have imagined. I've come to realize that what we do together in our congregations, organizations, and businesses can be strengthened by what I have learned in managing a cockpit of an airplane and navigating safely in flight. In fact, I'd like to suggest that if you are a congregational leader, lay or ordained, you are also made to fly. You may not be flying an actual plane, but you are directing the flight of a congregation, organization, family, or business simply by your participation in it. Your leadership matters.

Measuring Risk

When people hear that I am a pilot, they sometimes assume I am a risk-taker and an adrenaline junkie. They often say, "Wow, you must be a little crazy. I could never do that." What they don't realize is that, experientially, for me it's the exact opposite. Being a pilot taught me to manage risks because there is more at stake. The minute I approach the plane for my preflight, I am focused, disciplined, and fully present. I don't skip steps in my checklists. I double-check my calculations. I trust my training and my instincts. I take far fewer risks in my cockpit than I ever would walking down the street. I am a good pilot *precisely because I manage risk.*

Leadership will feel risky because it is the art of creating something that has never existed or doing something that has never been done. No one has ever renewed your congregation at this moment in history with the resources at your disposal. No one has ever tried to start a new ministry in your town, with your vision and with the people you have gathered. It might feel like a bigger risk than you can manage, but here is the key: do your homework, don't cut corners, trust your training. That is how you lead with excellence.

Take Responsibility for Your Possibility

Do you remember the story of Nehemiah, the cupbearer to King Artaxerxes? He visited Jerusalem and, seeing the walls of Jerusalem lying in ruins, decided that he needed to rebuild them. Can you imagine? He was the guy who tasted the food before the king to make sure it wasn't poisoned. He was not a mason. He didn't have formal training in wall-building. No one told him that the walls needed to be rebuilt and then gave him the task to do it. He saw that it needed to be done and took responsibility for making it happen. That's leadership.

It wasn't easy. He had to convince the king to let him go, organize the investors, disarm the militia, recruit the workers, convince the townspeople, and mobilize the support teams. I'm sure he had moments of doubt and wondered if he had lost his mind. But he took responsibility for their collective possibility. He knew that, with the help of so many others, he could rebuild that wall.

What if your congregation and its membership had extraordinary untapped potential within its walls? What if you actually *could* change the world...or at least your community? In congregations I work with across the nation, there are members who are exceptionally talented and well-connected professionals in their "day jobs." They are influencing our national policy, teaching our children, leading our cities, serving as CEOs and vice presidents of our Fortune 500 companies, changing the culture as technology innovators, caring for people as HR professionals, leading as project managers...so many talented people who work in fields that shape our world. But when they come to church, *rarely* are they asked to bring what they know and do in their professional fields into the mission of the church. Rarely are they asked to consider how their contribution to their industries can create a more just and generous world. Why? What could be possible if we did?

Millard Fuller was a lay member of the Christian Church (Disciples of Christ). He had a deep love for the church, but he never considered it a career path for himself. His passions were around business, economics, and law. By the time he was in his early twenties, he was already well on his way to a successful life. He was newly married and had recently completed his business and law degrees in Alabama. He was a self-made millionaire by the time he was 29 years old. But Millard and his wife Linda wanted to make a bigger difference for people in the world. They had become friends with Clarence Jordan, the founder of Koinonia Farms in southern Georgia, and decided to move there to be part of that intentional Christian community.

Millard and Linda began building simple, decent houses for low-income families in their community using volunteer labor and donations, and requiring repayment only of the cost of the materials used. No interest was charged, as it is with traditional mortgages, and no profit was made. The model proved sustainable and soon they formed a new organization called Habitat for Humanity. Millard went to the national offices of many of the major denominations at that time. His pitch was: "What if you became known as the Church that housed people?" No denominations took him up on the partnership. Millard then began courting a famous volunteer, President Jimmy Carter, whose affiliation took Habitat for Humanity from being a small NGO in southern Georgia to an international organization that has housed over a million people in 100 countries.

Millard and Linda Fuller were lay leaders with a vision for living out their Christian life at a grand scale. Their faith community gave them the space to test their concepts, but, ultimately, Millard and Linda had to decide they were going to take responsibility for bringing this vision into reality.

In aviation, we use the acronym D.E.C.I.D.E to frame critical pilot decisions:

D- Detect that the action is necessary;

E- Estimate the significance of the action;

C- Choose a desirable outcome;

I- Identify actions needed to achieve the chosen option;

D- Do the necessary action to achieve change;

E- Evaluate the effects of the action.

Taking responsibility for your possibility means that you *DECIDE* to do something about a challenge or opportunity. You choose to lead. Millard and Linda Fuller led us all forward in making the world a more just and generous place. Imagine if more denominations and churches had gotten behind them earlier. The Fullers taught us a valuable lesson: if we are willing to lean on the entirety of our gifts and collaborate broadly with others for the sake of a larger vision, there isn't a community challenge that we can't take on.

You're Getting Somewhere...

Early in my first congregation, I had the benefit of working with an executive from IBM who was committed to helping me level up my leadership. He accompanied me to a meeting with our leadership team during which we would be discussing a big decision we were facing about our future, and I was responsible for articulating a vision that could help us move forward. It was a big deal. A lot was at stake. And...I blew it. While my words were clear, my energy was passive. I failed to tap into the full potential of my influence. I let louder voices (literally) have more influence than they deserved. I passed over opportunities to advance the conversation. In the end, we came to a decision that was a faded copy of what I knew we were capable of as a team.

As we walked out of that meeting, I knew I had failed. I had prepared for that meeting, but walked in and choked. My coach, who was a tall 6'4" bald guy, turned to me in the parking lot and put his hands on my shoulders. Looking down into my eyes, he said, "Cameron, do you know what a giraffe is?" I looked at him, confused. He continued, "A giraffe is a horse designed by a committee. You just created a great big giraffe in there." He was right. I knew I would have to fix it. But he went on to say something that has stayed with me all this time. He said, "Remember this, Cameron. Everyone gets somewhere in life. The rare person gets somewhere on purpose." He was inviting me to be crystal clear in my vision for where we were going, and then be courageous enough to pilot us in that direction.

It's good wisdom for your congregation as well. Your congregation is going somewhere. It's spending lots of time and money on staffing, buildings, ministries, and community impact. The question is, are you going somewhere on purpose? Are you clear about the difference you are making and the difference you want to make? Are you measuring what matters? Are you shaping the kind of community, the kind of world, you want to see 10, 20, or 50 years from now?

Your leadership is what makes the difference. You are the pilot of that plane. You are in control in this one critical way: you have extraordinary influence over your church living fully into its potential. You can influence the size of your collective dreams. You can change your congregation's priorities by shaping the budget. You can expand your congregation's influence by promoting community partnerships. More critically, you don't need to be the pastor to have this influence. The kind of leadership that I am talking about and invested in cultivating in your church isn't dependent upon institutional authority. You are a leader when you choose to lead. You don't need permission.

Why Not You?

Carey Lohrenz is the US Navy's first female F-14 Tomcat fighter pilot. Growing up, she remembers playing with her father's old silk maps from his time flying in the Marine Corps in Vietnam. Even as a little girl, she knew she wanted to be a pilot. She also knew that she would need a huge dose of courage to make that happen. Being a female fighter pilot in the 1990s was simply unheard of. She didn't tell many people about her dreams in high school and college, but she was clear about where she was going.

In her book, *Fearless Leadership: High Performance Lessons from the Flight Deck* she talks about watching colleagues and fellow aviators fail to make the cut. She writes, "Pursuing leadership is highly a personal decision, and I've seen many people back away from great leadership opportunities, spouting lines like 'I'm not sure I'm ready' and 'I just think it's too soon' and 'I still have some growing to do.' These statements, though masquerading as neutral, are actually quite negative. They almost always mask insecurity and a desire to avoid the challenges that come with leadership. These statements are the fear talking—and it's saying self-defeating things."[2]

That voice of fear, saying all kinds of self-defeating things, has grabbed the ears of too many leaders in our congregations and denominations. I'm not sure when that started happening or why. Today, I find us dreaming such small dreams about the potential of our congregations. Likely because we are living through decades of decline and deconstruction, we perhaps have become convinced that what we have to offer doesn't matter. We are heroes if we can just keep our doors open. Or, maybe we are overwhelmed by the larger needs in our communities and don't know where to start with our dwindling resources. Whatever the story might be that we are telling ourselves, we are currently living in a time when our national, regional, and sometimes local congregational settings are too often dreaming small dreams.

I don't understand why.

Lohrenz quotes Dharmesh Shah, the cofounder and chief technology officer for HubSpot, who pointed out in a blog posting that a key leadership quality of effective leaders is to think: "Why *not* me?"[3]

Exactly! Why *not* you? Why *not* your church? Why *not* all of us making a difference for the sake of a more just and generous world?

Our communities need your congregations to lead in creating more loving neighbors, more generous civil servants, and more businesses offering meaningful employment. In fact, I can't think of a reason that we need so many churches in this world *unless* each of these churches is relentlessly committed to raising the standard of life for people living around them. If we are going to obsess about Sunday attendance and giving (institutional maintenance), we should also obsess about graduation rates, employment rates, and crime rates (community transformation).

Jesus taught us that sacred human life is fully integrated—our internal spiritual formation is tied to our external actions. Do you remember the stories of Jesus teaching all day to crowds who were so hungry to hear what he was saying that they ran out of food and stayed to hear him anyway? He knew both kinds of hunger mattered. He told his disciples to share their food; in the end, everyone had enough to eat. He did this more than once. His disciples grew frustrated. They didn't understand why they had to care about the physical well-being of these people. But Jesus reminded them that compassion is the path of discipleship, basically explaining: "We are one global family, all in this together." So, he said to the disciples, "What good would it do to get everything you want and lose you, the real you? What could you ever trade your soul for?"[4]

It might be possible that many congregations have gotten everything they wanted—the big fancy buildings, the accomplished clergy, the fun programs—and lost their very souls. Maybe your congregation is experiencing this, trying to remember why you exist as part of a larger story of transformation beyond institutional maintenance. All is not lost, if you are courageous enough to own your reality and act on it now.

You and your congregation can decide to come together to decide what difference you want to make in the world. When it feels too big, or too expensive, or like it should be someone else's responsibility, I want you to pause and ask, "Why *not* me?" My guess is that you are the leader we've been waiting for.

Sure It's Scary...So What?

When I stand on the stage in front of a group, I often ask one question: "What would you do if you were brave?" What would those in the audience do as individuals, as churches, as denominations if they knew they couldn't fail? What would be the biggest, boldest, and most faithful contribution they could make to the world we are creating together?

This question is hard for most of us. It's too abstract and too grandiose. Most of the time, people feel inspired and deflated at the same time. "Being brave" feels as if we should have some amazing coming of age story or some heroic tale of overcoming impending death in the face of every imaginable obstacle. I've now decided that this is how we hide. If bravery must look Hollywood worthy, then we can comfortably tell ourselves that the brave life is out of our reach. It's not meant to be.

Here is what bravery looks like: bravery is creativity in action.

Bravery is feeling all of the fear of change, of trying something new, of embracing new ideas, of exploring new terrain, of preaching new sermons, of embracing new relationships, of accepting new jobs, of singing new songs, of living in new places, of saying goodbye to what was and *still* making that change and embracing what can be.

Bravery is about taking the next best step, whatever that may be.

I know your fear because it is mine too. In fact, most of my coaching work with pastors and leaders involves confronting the fears that keep them paralyzed from acting on their greatest potential. Let's name a few:

...You're afraid people will figure out you have no idea what you are doing.

...You're afraid you aren't smart enough or creative enough or original enough.

...You're afraid people will question your right to lead them.

...You're afraid you will run out of money and be poor and destitute, living on the street.

...You're afraid people will see through your "act."

...You're afraid your leaders will think you're stupid.

...You're afraid people will reject your ministry and not come to church.

...You're afraid people will judge your weight.

...You're afraid your children will grow up hating church.

...You're afraid your children will grow up hating you.

...You're afraid your friends will gossip about you.

...You're afraid your work isn't good enough.

...You're afraid your ambition is arrogant.

...You're afraid your dreams are silly.

...You're afraid you are wasting your life.

...You're afraid your family will disown you if you tell them who you truly love.

...You're afraid you will lose your job if you are honest about your wavering faith.

...You're afraid you are not producing enough.

...You're afraid you are not organized enough.

...You're afraid you are too old.

...You're afraid it's too late.

...You're afraid your best effort won't be good enough.

...You're afraid if you commit to something it might not be as good as what could come next.

...You're afraid your denomination is dying and none of this matters.

...You're afraid no one wants to hear what you have to say.

...You're afraid you don't have anything to say worth hearing.

...You're afraid...

I get it. We all get it. We all struggle with doubt, fear, and negative self-talk that threatens to kill the creative bravery within every one of us. So, before we go any further, let's deal with this.

Hear me: You're scared. So what? What is the worst thing that could possibly happen? What is the worst, most horrible outcome that you can imagine? Now, think about the best and most wonderful outcome. What does that look like and feel like? What is a moderate outcome, one in which you don't save the world but you don't die either? Can you sense that? Do you see it?

Now, feel all of the feelings. Let them run through you. And then move on. Feelings are physical experiences that last about 90 seconds in our bodies. They are chemical reactions that drive hormonal changes in our bodies. If you let the *feelings of fear* pass through you without triggering you, you return to a place of balance and deeper wisdom. You can take the next best step from this space, the space beyond fear-filled feelings.

Because fear immobilizes our power and impact, fear is probably the greatest stumbling block to God's work in the world. It might manifest in fear of change, a fear of killing your church, a fear of being ridiculed, a fear of death, a fear of failure, or maybe even fear of success. Fear makes us "hold on" when all signs tell us that we should "let go." This is the problem with fear: it prevents us from letting go of what "is" so that something new might come.

So, feel the fear. But never let it stop you. Never let it make your decisions for you. Too much is at stake in your offering of your fullest self to a world that really needs you to show up.

A Personal Practice: Vision Board

When I was in my early twenties, I began a practice that has literally changed my life. I read an article by psychologist and coach Dr. Martha Beck about creating a "vision board."[5] The idea is simple: look online or in magazines and find pictures that speak to the kind of life you want to lead/see/embody in the coming year. Print or cut those pictures out and paste them on a poster board. You can also create a collage on your computer and then print out a single sheet. Then, put that board or printed sheet in a prominent place where you see it every day.

I created my first vision board when I was twenty-two. I was married and transitioning as a pastor and denominational leader into an entirely new denomination. I was also working in the for-profit sector and trying to figure out what I really wanted to do with my life. I was a *young* woman working in systems historically dominated by older white men. I was Southern, joining a denomination based in New England. I was absurdly entrepreneurial, trying to work in deeply institutional systems. It was a lot.

I sat down at the beginning of each year and dreamed about what could be possible. I added a picture of a church because I wanted to serve as a pastor in a local congregation. I added a picture of a business because I also wanted to run a company. I added a picture of an airplane because I wanted to fly and see the world. I added a picture of my family because I wanted to be a good wife, mother, sister, niece, and daughter. I added a picture of the United Nations because I wanted to work on major world problems through major global systems. I added a picture of a woman who was physically fit because I wanted to take care of my body. I added...well, you get the point.

Every day, I looked at the vision of my possible life. Every day, I believed just a little more that I could be, do, and have those things that I dreamed of. Every day, I trusted that my hopes would be stronger than my fears.

Your turn: Thinking about the next 12 months of your life...

Name three people you think of as brave and explain why. (What have they done? What drove them?)

1. _____

2. _____

3. _____

Name three experiences you want to have. Go big here.

1. _____

2. _____

3. _____

Name three professional goals you want to accomplish.

1. _____

2. _____

3. _____

Name three personal goals you want to accomplish.

1. _____

2. _____

3. _____

Name three people you want to meet who could help you accomplish your goals.

1. _____

2. _____

3. _____

Now that you have a sense of where you want to go, it's time to start taking steps to get there. We will get to how to do that soon. For now, all you need to think about is, "What is my next best step?" You don't need to know *all* of the steps. You just need to know the *next* one. What is it? Now, go do it!

A Congregational Practice: Impact Board

Make a list of all the activities that you all have led or participated in as a congregation this past year. Use lots of Post-It notes (just because they are awesome), and stick all the activities on a wall. Now, step back and ask these questions about each: *What difference did it make? How did it change your community? How did it help you all grow into more loving people?*

Next, let's understand the value of your collective leadership. On a flip chart, list each activity and estimate the number of hours each volunteer dedicated to each particular project/ministry/action. Add all those up into one huge number. Then multiply that number by $7.25 (the current nationally mandated minimum wage in the United States).

Example: Total Volunteer Hours (8,000) x Minimum Wage ($7.25) = $58,000

That number is the cash value of the investment you as a congregation have made to your church and your community. Did you know? I bet in your case, it's a big number. I hope you celebrate it. You are making a real difference in the world. Keep it up!

Small Group Discussion Questions

1. What is your congregation doing that you think matters? What difference is it making?

2. What are you as a congregation afraid to do?

3. How would you define the values of your church?

4. What needs to be done in your community that no one is doing?

5. Imagine that it is five years from today. What would you like to be able to say about your leadership in your congregation? What can it count on you to contribute? What is holding your congregation back?

[1] See https://www.faa.gov/data_research/aviation_data_statistics/civil_airmen_statistics.

[2] Carey D. Lohrenz, *Fearless Leadership: High Performance Lessons from the Flight Deck* (Austin, Texas: Greenleaf Books, 2014), 25.

[3] Ibid.

[4] Mark 8:36–37, *The Message.*

[5] Martha Beck, "How To Make A Vision Board: Find Your Life Ambition," Martha Beck blog, https://marthabeck.com/tag/vision-board/ .

Chapter Two

What Kind of Pilot Will You Be?

Checklist

☐ Commit to personal practices that help you stay healthy

☐ See your therapist, just for good measure

☐ Take some personality assessments to understand your unique triggers and fears

☐ Complete your physical exam required by the FAA

"Fighter pilot is not just a description, it's an attitude: it's cockiness, it's aggressiveness, it's self-confidence. It is a streak of rebelliousness and competitiveness. But there's something else; there's a spark. There's a desire to be good, to do well; in the eyes of your peers, and in your own mind." [1]
—*Robin Olds, American fighter pilot and later Brigadier General in the U.S. Air Force*

Do you know how you learn to fly? You do it. Your very first lesson is in the cockpit flying an actual plane. I assumed that I would spend hours in ground school, learning the basics of aerodynamics, weather, communications, airplane parts...all those things. But nope. Your flight instructor puts you in a plane and goes over a few basics—such as where the yoke is and what your rudder pedals actually do. Then, he taxis to the runway, looks over at you, and says, "Your controls."

That was the first moment I began to wonder what kind of pilot I would be. I did a double-take as my instructor, Jim, just stared at me. "Is he serious?" I thought. "He does know I don't really know what I am doing, right? I could actually kill us... Whatever. It's been a good life." I took a deep breath, gripped the yoke, pushed the throttle forward and watched as my speed climbed slowly...27 knots, 39 knots, 46 knots, 57 knots—Bingo! Fifty-seven knots is my rotation speed. Gently, I pulled back on the yoke... and that tiny little plane actually took off. I couldn't believe it! I nearly dislocated my jaw from the huge grin that spread across my face. "My God!" I thought, "I am flying!"

Do You Have What It Takes?

The first step to becoming a pilot is being brave enough to climb in the cockpit in the first place. That is also certainly true of becoming a faith leader. The first step is being brave enough to climb into that pulpit or sit in that pew or join that community. Once you are there, you are signaling to the world that you are committed. You are showing up and taking responsibility for what you contribute to the flight you are charting together.

The second step is having the personal discipline and integrity to do the professional and self-development work to stay there. You don't graduate with your pilot's license and then never have to attend more ground school or complete another check ride again. Flying is a lifestyle, and being a pilot is a way of life. When I talk about my commitment to flying, I say, "I am a pilot." I don't say, "I like to pilot," or, "I'm going piloting tomorrow." I make an identity statement. "I am a pilot" is a way of *being* in the world. I am never *NOT* being a pilot. Because I am a pilot, every day I pay attention to the weather, I study new plane technology, I care about my personal fitness and nutrition, I stay up to date on the latest FAA regulation changes or recommendations, and I connect to other pilots to learn from their experiences. Being a pilot means I have adopted a discipline that ensures that I continue to grow in my learning and develop the skills to make me a safe (and fun!) aviatrix.

You are a leader. You are not engaging in leadership on occasion. You are a leader every minute of every day. Being a leader is the way you are in the world; it's an identity. With that comes a recognition that you owe it to yourself and those who follow you to adopt the daily disciplines that improve your skills, sharpen your focus, and deepen your influence. As a faith leader, you have a special opportunity as one who can help people see how their lives connect to a larger story of humanity and a common sacred Love that unites us all. When we live life feeling separated from other people, we suffer. But when we realize that we are connected, interdependent with one another and our planet, we thrive in our potential to shape a better world for all.

The Pro and the Amateur

Since the Wright Brothers took off at Kitty Hawk, North Carolina, in 1903, aviation has expanded to include an average of 550,000 active pilots[2] in any given year in the United States. If I asked you to name some of those current pilots, you might be hard-pressed. You could probably name some pilots of previous generations—people such as Chuck Yeager, Amelia Earhart, and Charles A. Lindbergh. You might also remember a modern aviation hero, Sully Sullenberger, Captain of US Airways Flight 1549, who on January 15, 2009, safely landed a crippled Airbus 320 filled with 155 people in the middle of the Hudson River in New York. You've heard of these people because they accomplished feats that to the rest of us seem extraordinary. They made history.

Oddly, though, when you listen to the interviews with these pilots about their experiences, you hear them talk about how the daily practice of flying, the discipline of practicing day after day, prepared them for the extraordinary event that ultimately made them famous. Captain Sullenberger said it this way: "For 42 years, I've been making small, regular deposits in this bank of experience, education and training. And on January 15, the balance was sufficient so that I could make a very large withdrawal."[3] In his case, when potential tragedy struck, he was prepared to rise to the challenge. He was ready to lead.

These pilots are professionals. They live and breathe their craft. They train at the highest levels, pushing themselves to be smarter, faster, and wiser as part of the commitment they have had to their profession. They approach flying with the same discipline that a professional athlete approaches his or her training. They get up early in the mornings thinking about flying. They don't skip steps on their preflight inspections. They don't disregard steps in their standard checklists. They aren't casual in their communication with ATC (Air Traffic Control). They debrief after each flight to learn what they can improve for the next. They log simulator time to prepare for any imaginable scenario. They think about their nutrition and fitness, and complete regular medical exams. They want to be the best, to play at the highest level of their ability. It's who they are.

They also tend to befriend others similar to them. They surround themselves with others who share their level of commitment. They know that playing with other "pros" makes them push themselves harder. Even if you are an average player, you are likely to play basketball at a higher level if you are playing with Lebron James.

We can point to a handful of faith leaders today who we recognize as having that same level of dedication to their own growth. One of my clients, a man named David, was serving a congregation as the new senior minister. You could tell that every cell in his body was made to serve the world this way. He woke up thinking about how to lead the congregation and engage the community. He prayed and studied in the mornings before his kids awoke. During the day he watched people carefully, listening to what they were (and were not) saying. He had an uncanny ability to tell stories that helped people see insights they might miss. He cared about how their staff team shaped the Sunday morning worship experience and spent much of his best energy planning the service and writing his sermons. He understood how to create infrastructure and systems that helped the church to grow. He was not casual about his leadership in this church; he was in the business of creating a thriving congregation that made the world a more loving place. Not surprisingly, he developed friendships with other colleagues around the nation who are known for the scale and impact of their ministries. They all share a competitive and collaborative energy that drives them to be at their best. Their churches reflect their dedication—they are growing, thriving, and making a difference.

We need more leaders like David. We need more lay leaders and pastors who are clear about the difference they are trying to make and set out to live into that regardless of the cost. We need more "pro players" in the faith space willing to step up and make a difference in our communities and our world. With the state of the world, so much is at stake.

Our other option, of course, is to play at the amateur level. I am an amateur at a lot of things—I am an amateur tennis player, an amateur CrossFitter, an amateur chef. The difference, of course, is that I don't get up in the mornings thinking about my tennis game or wondering if I'll break a personal weightlifting record or working on designing a new "foodie dish." I just stretch a bit before I walk onto the court and hit balls. I might jog a bit before lifting weights to make sure I am warmed up. I throw some things in a pot for dinner and hope for the best. Because of that, I am never going to play at the professional level of any of these activities. I am not doing the things that make me a pro.

What Makes a Pro?

Todd Shellnut, my current flight instructor, looked at me over the rims of his glasses as we sat in the conference room at the airport reviewing my ground school material. "Tell me," he said, "what is the regulation defined in FAR 14 CFR 91.205?" I just stared at him. He did this to me a lot. The FAA publishes a 1000-page book called the Federal Aviation Regulations (FAR) with really tiny typed regulations filling each page. There are millions of them. As commercial and instrument-rated pilots, we need to know basically all of them—and Todd actually does. I could say to him, "Hey Todd, tell me what 61.113 says," and he could spout it off.

"I have no idea, Todd," I sheepishly confess. I couldn't imagine that I needed to know all of this. Isn't that why we have books where we can look things up? But then it dawned on me. *Professional* pilots know the regulations. *Amateurs* look them up. Todd is committed to making me a professional. He is always looking for signs that prove I have what it takes.

What does it take? I've interviewed pastors and lay leaders in the past four years asking that very question. What does it take to embody inspiring, visionary, faith-filled leadership with which we can reshape our world for the better? I've heard things such as:

"It takes more than pretty sermons. You have to meet people where they are and help them see the difference they can make."

"You have to believe. You have to believe in grace and hope and resurrection. But you also have to believe in pain and death. The hells on earth are powerful motivators."

"I think you're born with a gift for leadership...or you aren't. I don't think it can be taught and be powerful."

"It takes years of practicing the faith. You really have to live it and let it change you. People can see that change in you and it inspires change in them."

These are helpful insights. But what I observed about these leaders taught me even more. The difference their ministry was making seemed to be related to how committed they were to their own self-development. The more they acted, talked, and walked like Jesus, the more powerful their leadership. I could predict that they moved in the world with these qualities:

Courage

Not the kind of courage evidenced only by heroic acts or great feats, but the kind of courage that points to an inner strength of character. Brené Brown says it best when she writes, "Courage is a heart word. The root of the word *courage* is *cor*—the Latin word for heart. In one of its earliest forms, the word *courage* meant 'To speak one's mind by telling all one's heart.'"[4] These leaders have an inner courage that allows for "heart-driven" emotional transparency that nearly takes your breath away. They are living *whole-hearted* lives. They know who they are. They know what they are committed to. They are courageous enough to offer it to the world, willing to risk rejection and failure in the process. But they are relentlessly real. I don't know what could be more courageous.

Authenticity

I define authenticity as being entirely comfortable with being who you are without the need to justify or explain or pretend. I remember a beautiful conversation with Abby, a church leader in Phoenix, Arizona, telling me about her struggles with addiction. She said, "Look, I am so far from perfect. I can tell you about how drugs can become more important than food. I can tell you about lying to people I love just to get my next fix. I can tell you about desperate times and times I wanted to die. I've been broken and put back together so many times that God is turning me into something entirely new and far more beautiful. I wouldn't trade anything for the journey...except some of the pain I've caused others." She didn't justify her actions. She didn't gloss over them. She told me the truth about her life...and it was beautiful. Today, when Abby speaks at community rallies or preaches sermons and talks about grace, pain, suffering, losing herself, finding herself, and resurrection, we know that she knows what she is talking about. She is the real deal, and inspires the rest of us to cherish the broken and mended places in ourselves just a bit more, because those are the signs of God's grace in our lives.

Resilience

I saw this characteristic in these leaders perhaps more than anything else. These people can get knocked down, but they get right back up. They remind me of that game I used to play as a child called "Whac-A-Mole." You would "whack" the "moles" down into their holes, and then they'd pop right back up! Sometimes I wondered if they even knew they had been hit at all. Of course, they wanted me to wonder; appearing unfazed or uninjured is part of the gift. But the longer I do this work, the more I marvel at this capacity. Every industry can be challenging, but the faith sector can be particularly cruel. We are the people who are supposed to be kind, compassionate, and graceful with one another. Yet, far too often, we target our leaders with gossip, critique, and political games under the guise of Christian love. I've watched many of our national leaders forced into spending too much time defending themselves against their own colleagues at the sacrifice of the work they were called to do in the first place. Yet they keep pushing forward. They keep announcing hope.

In May of 2003, Hara Estroff Marano, editor of *Psychology Today*, published an article called "The Art of Resilience," in which she observed: "Resilient people do not let adversity define them. They find resilience by moving towards a goal beyond themselves, transcending pain and grief by perceiving bad times as a temporary state of affairs... It's possible to strengthen your inner self and your belief in yourself, to define yourself as capable and competent. It's possible to fortify your psyche. It's possible to develop a sense of mastery."[5] For resilient leaders, their sense of inner strength is undeniable and unwavering. They are committed to broader goals.

Theological Imagination

Of all the traits, this is one I find to be the most inspiring. These leaders have a particular capacity—a kind of imagination—that allows them to see what "heaven on earth" might actually look like and, then, how we might create it together. When they look at the world, it is almost as if they can hear the old biblical stories playing in their ears, with the nuggets of wisdom hidden in them coming alive once again in this age. One morning, I had breakfast with Laura, a pastor of a large congregation in Atlanta. Toward the end of the conversation, she paused, leaned across the table, and *whispered*—almost as if she was worried I would think she had lost her mind completely—"I have a crazy, huge dream of what our church could be in the world." She then went on to outline one of the most exciting, visionary strategies that I have ever heard from a pastor. By the time she finished talking, I was ready to quit my job and sign up to help. She *must* succeed. The world needs this kind of church to exist. I drove back to the office pondering what it would be like if more of us had that kind of imagination for our possibility. I would love to live in such a place.

The power of theological imagination is its capacity to energize people in congregations to acts of exceptional bravery and compassion as part of a longer, larger story of God walking with us and working through us for a better world. When we understand our actions as part of an unfolding narrative of Love, we can do anything. We can imagine heaven on earth, we can address global poverty, we can solve the climate crisis. We simply need an imagination creative enough to see it into being.

Connection

I could also call this "collaboration," because they seem to go hand in hand. They understood what Adrienne Brown highlights in her book *Emergent Strategy*[6]: Progress happens at the speed of trust. We have to trust one another to work together. Trust only comes through authentic connection. And how do we make an authentic connection with those around us? We let go of who we think we should be, and just be who we are. When we are honest about who we are, we become trust-worthy. In that space, opportunities for connection and collaboration open to us.

Activist Spirit

Camille is a pastor in New York serving a congregation of Wall Street bankers, high-powered senior level executives, homeless people, and undocumented immigrants. Every Sunday in her pews, the homeless man and the Wall Street executive pass the peace to one another, greeting each other in the name of Jesus during the service. "Where else would this ever happen?" Camille asks. "Here, for one hour on Sunday, we are all valued. We are all equal. We are all in the same sacred family. It's the most beautiful thing I have ever seen in my ministry."

Over the past few months, they started noticing that more and more of their immigrant families were not coming to church. When Camille started reaching out to them, she discovered to her horror that many of them were being arrested and detained by ICE officials because they were undocumented. Her congregants, who had lived in New York for dozens of years, were being held in jail without a trial or resources to push for their release. When Camille reported this to her church leaders, there was an uprising. The leaders of the church mobilized almost overnight, hiring immigration attorneys, attending hearings, and holding press conferences. They launched a social media campaign to tell the story of what was happening in New York and issued a national call to action for other churches to join the fight—in New York, and in their own communities.

The saga continues as I write these pages. They have secured the release of almost all of their congregants, but in the process learned of so many more being held indefinitely. They are now a congregation on a mission, advocating for those who can't advocate for themselves. It's that activist spirit that drives them to make the world a more just and generous place. May they inspire us all.

A Deep Faith

The reason I list this last is because it is the most important—it's the foundation of everything that has come before. These leaders really believe that God is with us. They really believe that prayer matters. They really believe that life and death, and life again, is the natural rhythm of the world. They really believe that God is real, the Church matters, and we can make this world feel a little more like heaven if we become more loving people. They aren't agnostic about any of this; they know these truths in the core of their bones. Their faith is so deep and so solid that it fuels their every breath, and the rest of us can see it emanate from them.

Mother Teresa was often questioned about her commitment to the poor in India. People wanted her to explain why she cared and why they should care too. Over and over she was interviewed and interrogated about how her faith drove her to make such sacrifice. Finally, tired of trying to explain, she simply said, "Too many words. Let them see how we live." Certainly, for these leaders that I talked to, I could see how they lived and knew that it changed everything.

What about You?

What kind of pilot will you be? I hope one that embodies all of the qualities I've named and adds more to that list. Most of us have a natural energetic pattern, an instinct that serves as our ground of being. Our friends and family *sense* our energy more than intellectually diagnose it. We observe it in ourselves as an authentic expression of "me." Below, I've outlined a few common leadership profiles that may spark some sense of self-recognition. While undoubtedly you don't want to be the second type pilot in any of these scenarios, if you recognize yourself in the descriptions, maybe it's time for changes. In reading through them, note what comes up for you—what feels right? What feels off? Is there one type of "pilot" that really sums up your essence? Or, do you feel yourself to be a blend of a few?

Activist Pilot or Ambivalent Pilot	
Activist Pilots are those who see opportunity, injustice, or danger, and act to engage. They can fire people up, are great motivators, and often see issues the rest of us miss. They can also move too quickly, alienating the team or organizational partners.	
Ambivalent Pilots are those who see opportunity, injustice, or danger, and justify reasons for not engaging. They are place-holders in systems, moved to action only when their direct self-interest is threatened.	
Behaviors of the Activist Pilot	
• Self-assertive, self-confident • Driven by compassion for people suffering from injustice, and by creative anger at systems that disenfranchise them • Action-oriented • Direct communicators • Use power constructively to champion the protection of people and the planet	Inspirational Directive Collaborative
Behaviors of the Ambivalent Pilot	
• Go-it-alone mentality that can't partner well with other colleagues or organizations • Self-protective and emotionally defended • Believe the world is out to get them • Hate being challenged or cornered and will lash out at anyone/anything they perceive as trying to control them	Self-Centered Intimidating Cruel

Committed Pilot or Auto-Pilot		
Committed Pilots are warm, friendly, and engaging. They are highly responsible and trustworthy. They are hard-working, dependable, and loyal to the people and the causes they invest in. They can also struggle with self-doubt, which can sometimes cause them to want to "cover the bases."		
Auto-Pilots are those who are retired in place. They are ambivalent about the outcome of projects or the organizations they lead. They will not act or offer leadership unless forced to by crisis circumstances. They lack initiative and can be highly resistant if pushed to change.		
Behaviors of the Committed Pilot		
• Warm, engaging, and trustworthy • Loyal to the people and causes they commit to supporting • Inner-directed and can be trusted to follow through on what they have said they will do • Egalitarian spirit • Care about the quality of their work	Self-Reliant Engaged Cooperative	
Behaviors of the Auto-Pilot		
• General agnosticism masks a deep fear or anxiety that they are irrelevant or inferior • Suspicious of anyone or anything that challenges their established patterns • Look to others to rescue them while promoting a narrative of defenselessness	Cowardly Indecisive Suspicious	

Collaborative Pilot or Cocky Pilot
Collaborative Pilots are stable, receptive, open, and accepting. They enjoy working in groups and are patient with their teammates. They generally have easy-going personalities and prefer to keep things simple. They have a calming presence when needed but can also be powerful and dynamic when they need to be. They can be conflict-adverse, which can create problems with their teams over time.
Cocky Pilots are those who give the appearance of "having it all together." They reject anything that does not support their self-image. They can be dismissive of their team and lazy when it comes to performance. Because they don't solicit feedback and input from others, they can have significant blind spots that can undermine their work/relationships. When they fail, they will become angry at themselves secretly, and others publicly.

Behaviors of the Collaborative Pilot	
• Grounded in a clear sense of self and project an open spirit that draws people to them • They are often fun to be around, offering genuine kindness to those in their social networks • They are unpretentious and enjoy bringing people together	Generous Adaptable Sensitive to others
Behaviors of the Cocky Pilot	
• Only work with people who buy into and affirm their self-image • Self-absorbed and temperamental • Action is focused on self-aggrandizement or ego • Can take unreasonable risks to "save face" • Scared that people will see who they really are and find them lacking in some way	Temperamental Self-indulgent Alienating

Maverick Pilot or Risk-Averse Pilot	
Maverick Pilots are self-assertive and confidant. They are often divergent thinkers who ask "why" instead of simply accepting the norm. They can be tenacious when they set their minds to accomplishing a task, usually valuing independence and fostering it in others. They are decisive and commanding leaders. They can also be domineering and bossy when others do not do something "their way."	
Risk-Averse Pilots are those who calculate risk before reward. They are driven by a fear that they will make a fatal error from which they cannot return. They can often paralyze themselves with analysis paralysis. They struggle to make decisions and isolate themselves if they feel pressured to move too quickly by others.	
Behavior of the Maverick Pilot	
• Self-expressive and willing to take risks others might deem too extreme • Profoundly creative • Passionate in their work and personal relationships • Powerful imagination • Individualistic	Adventurous Strong Courageous

Behavior of the Risk-Averse Pilot	
• They are often binary in their thinking—right and wrong, good and bad, black and white • They can be dogmatic, close-minded, and inflexible when pushed to move faster than they care to • They can easily become bitter and depressed if others do not heed their calls for caution	Cautious Passive Disassociated

Inspiring Pilot or Hopeless Pilot	
Inspiring Pilots are high-spirited, energetic, and often charming and popular. They are usually truly admirable in some way, striving to be the best that they can be. They are excellent communicators, motivators and promoters. They are genuine and authentic. When they lose their center, they fear humiliation and can be exploitive and opportunistic. **Hopeless Pilots** struggle with feelings of being unappreciated. They have naturally negative personalities, usually defaulting to why something won't work instead of why it might. They are adept at using guilt to influence others. At their core, they are afraid that their contributions do not make a difference. Rather than change their limiting belief or work harder, they live into that prophesy, making it hard to deny.	
Behaviors of the Inspiring Pilot	
• Enjoying high self-esteem, they help others see their own value and talents • They are good communicators, delivering messages of hope for the future • They motivate people to achieve more than they dreamed possible	Ambitious Adaptable Image conscious
Behaviors of the Hopeless Pilot	
• Default reaction to new ideas tends to be negative before they can find a positive perspective • Can be emotionally needy but unable to admit it • Can come across as dismissive, patronizing, and overbearing • May abuse food and alcohol to suppress feelings of inadequacy	Depressive Manipulative Victim mentality

What kind of pilot are you? What about your team members? What about your spouse? Likely you are a combination of all of these, depending on the day. The more interesting question is: At what level, professional or amateur, you are striving to lead? Are you happy with your performance? Do you need to level up? Let's explore that further.

A Personal Practice: Your Piloting Style

For this exercise we will use a scale to expand our awareness of our leadership instincts. As you look down the list, how might you rank yourself?

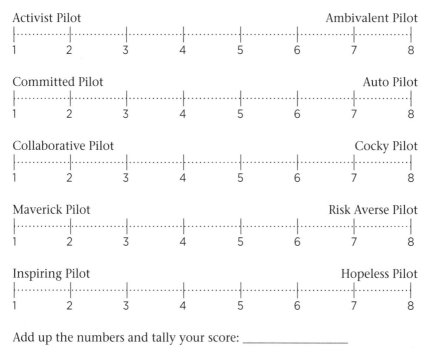

Add up the numbers and tally your score: _____

- ❏ *If you scored between 5 and 15, you are a pro leader. You are invested in your skill development, comfortable with your instincts, and feel natural in leadership positions. You were born for this!*

- ❏ *If you scored between 16 and 30, you tend to play to the moderates. You don't love to rock the boat but might if you felt it essential to maintaining the church. You might want to challenge yourself going forward to take more risks and consider what actions you might take that both make a* difference *and* accelerate *the change you are committed to making.*

- ❏ *If you scored between 31 and 40, you play it safe. Your heart may not be fully engaged and therefore the challenges of leadership are not interesting or worth it to you. You would benefit from considering what changes you could make in your leadership or your vocation that would align you with your highest capacities.*

A Congregational Practice

Now, let's consider your congregation. Your church culture establishes a "personality" that honors some behaviors and rebels against others. When you think about your experience as a member of your church, how would you rank your church?

On the whole we are...

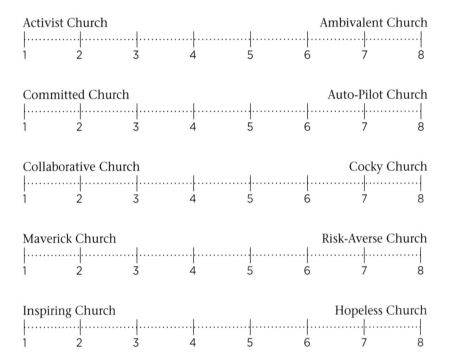

Activist Church   Ambivalent Church
1   2   3   4   5   6   7   8

Committed Church   Auto-Pilot Church
1   2   3   4   5   6   7   8

Collaborative Church   Cocky Church
1   2   3   4   5   6   7   8

Maverick Church   Risk-Averse Church
1   2   3   4   5   6   7   8

Inspiring Church   Hopeless Church
1   2   3   4   5   6   7   8

Have your congregation members complete this survey in small groups or during a congregational meeting as a creative exercise. Collect the responses, add them up and then determine the average.

Your average score for the group: 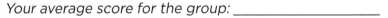 _____

❏ *If you scored between 5 and 15, you are a vital and courageous congregation. You are passionate about the difference you are making in the world and likely to wish that you could do even more. You understand the power of partnerships and work collaboratively with other organizations and congregations in your community. You empower leaders in your congregation to lead and reward new ideas. You are relevant, care about the issues of the day, and are clear about your theological calling to bring about a more just world.*

❏ *If you scored between 16 and 30, you are a congregation who tends to play it safe. You have people in the congregation that members don't want to upset, so those in leadership positions moderate ministries and actions. If a few people get upset, you as a congregation are likely to let their voices have influence and power. Most members want church to be a place where everyone is comfortable, so members avoid talking about tough issues until they are pushed. You might challenge yourself going forward to take more risks and consider what actions you might take as a congregation that both make a difference in the community and accelerate the change you are committed to making.*

❏ *If you scored between 31 and 40, you are a congregation who plays it safe. Members think church should be a place where you reconnect with friends and hear a good sermon that doesn't mention anything controversial. The ministries of the church are the ones that the congregation has had for years, though you are all getting worn out by running them year after year. Most members don't entirely recognize the world we are living in now, so church is a safe haven for them, a place that doesn't change in a world that is endlessly in flux.*

Perhaps you might diagnose your context differently. What would you add? What felt off? In looking at the individual responses of those willing to share, what do you all observe? What about the results makes you uncomfortable? What makes you proud? What might you want to shift? If you have the time, you could split each one of these binaries into a multi-week small group series for even further exploration. In these groups, you might consider how your congregation can move more toward the left side of these scales.

Small Group Discussion Questions

1. How does your personal style assessment match the church style assessment? How is it incongruent?

2. Did you discover anything in the aggregated congregational responses that you believe you all should work on together? Are you risk-averse in ways that are harming your mission? Are you on auto-pilot?

3. What would be the ideal balance for your congregation?

4. Do you believe you are invited to bring your best skills and style freely to the congregation's work and mission? Is there a more authentic expression of yourself that you like to offer as a leader in church?

5. Are you proud of your church and the difference it's making?

[1] Robin Olds, with Ed Rasimus and Christina Olds, *Fighter Pilot: The Memoirs of Legendary Ace Robin Olds* (New York: St. Martin's, 2010), 291.

[2] See https://en.wikipedia.org/wiki/Pilot_certification_in_the_United_States

[3] Chesley "Sully" Sullenberger, as quoted in Bill Newcott, "Wisdom of the Elders," *AARP Magazine* 347 (May–June 2009): 52.

[4] Brené Brown, *I Thought It Was Just Me (But It Isn't): Making the Journey from "What Will People Think?" to "I Am Enough"* (New York: Gotham Books, 2007), xxiii.

[5] https://www.psychologytoday.com/us/blog/design-your-path/201305/10-traits-emotionally-resilient-people.

[6] Adrienne Maree Brown, *Emergent Strategy: Shaping Change, Changing Worlds* (Chico, Calif.: AK Press, 2017).

Chapter Three

The Fundamentals of Flight

Checklist

- ☐ Learn the basics of lift, drag, weight, and thrust
- ☐ Test the limits of your plane by practicing maneuvers
- ☐ Factor in dew point and temperature when doing your weight and balance calculations
- ☐ Be prepared for anything.

"The engine is the heart of an airplane, but the pilot is its soul."
—Walter Alexander Raleigh (1861–1922)

Captain Tammie Jo Shults was the captain of Southwest Airline Flight 1380 from New York to Dallas. With 144 passengers onboard, she taxied the plane from the gate to the hold point just before entering the active runway and handing the controls over to her first officer for the takeoff. In commercial aviation, the captain and first officer trade flying responsibilities on each leg of the flights for the day. The takeoff was textbook, and they settled in for a cruising altitude at 32,000 feet.

Twenty minutes into the flight all hell broke loose. A metal blade from an engine broke apart, destroying the rest of that engine within seconds. The loose shrapnel pummeled the side of the cabin compartment of the plane, shattering a window and depressurizing the cabin. The plane yawed sharply to the left as Captain Shults called to the air traffic controllers: "Southwest 1380 has an engine fire." With not a hint of alarm in her voice, she added, "Descending." As she regained control, she began a rapid descent to 10,000 feet, a safe altitude where the passengers could breathe without the assistance of oxygen masks. For the next 40 minutes, she displayed what one passenger later called "nerves of steel," maneuvering the plane toward Philadelphia for an emergency landing. In an interview in the following days, Captain Shults reflected on the experience, "When you have altitude and ideas, you're okay. We had both." From her perspective, after years of training in the military and commercial aviation, this was a textbook emergency landing. No sweat. She's a genuine pro.

The starting place in learning to fly is with "flight fundamentals." That's literally what it's called in the books. At every moment of your flight, you have four forces acting on your aircraft at any moment:

- Thrust: the energy created by the engine that moves the plane forward. Thrust balances drag.

- Drag: the force created by the friction of the wind and air against the plane that holds the plane back. Drag balances thrust.

- Weight: the force, also called gravity, that pulls your plane toward the ground based on how much it weighs. Weight balances lift.

- Lift: the force generated by the wings and opposes weight. When lift is greater than weight, the airplane climbs. When lift is less than weight, the airplane descends. When lift and weight are equal, the airplane maintains its altitude. Lift balances weight.

These forces impact how fast you fly, how much fuel you burn, and how far you might drift off course without correction. To fly efficiently, these forces work in balance to give you a stable, uneventful flight. But when one or more of them dominates another, you will quickly find yourself in for a potentially wild ride.

When you are leading a congregation, you are tasked with understanding the performance dynamics of your church. When working in balance, congregational fundamentals such as *vision, mission, strategy,* and *culture* ensure a powerful future for your church. When they are out of balance, they cause strategic misalignment and systemic stress. At worst, they lead to a full system crash. You know these stories all too well: the church who runs off its pastor when she/he tries to change the worship service; the stalwart generation who refuses to embrace the ideas of the newer folks in the church; the demanding church member who bullies others to get their way. These are the stories that make people stop going to church. Who can blame them?

Your job is understanding the fundamentals of congregational leadership such that you can use these forces to promote health and growth in your church. To do this, you need to understand how they work at each phase of "flight." I've done extensive writing about the organizational lifecycle, which you can read about in my previous work.[1] Here I offer an adapted version in the hopes that it helps you see the influences available to you in your day-to-day leadership. Let's dig into this.

The Lifecycle

When I talk about organizational lifecycles, I frequently use the image of a standard bell curve, walking through the life/death cycle that is the natural rhythm of our world. Just as you and I experience birth, growth, decline, and death, so do the organizations we create. At each stage of our life, our perceptions, goals, needs, and challenges change as we adapt to the changes in our world and develop greater capacities within ourselves. These changes—both personally and organizationally—can be diagrammed effectively on a standard bell curve:

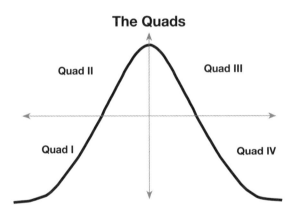

Every organization experiences growth and decline. These stages are marked by certain milestones that point to changes in organizational health and development. To better understand this, we use two lines of reference drawn in the shape of a cross through the middle of the curve. A vertical "Line of Vitality" represents either the numeric growth on the left side of the line, or the decline of the church on the right side of the line. The horizontal "Line of Sustainability" represents the financial health of the church, with those ministries below the line being dependent on denominational funding (or funding beyond the giving levels of active participants) and those above the line being sustained primarily through participant giving. These lines divide the church lifecycle into four quadrants: new, growth, decline, and dying. Each of these quadrants represents very different stages and requires different leadership skills, resources, ministries, strategies, and possibilities.

Understanding where your church is on this lifecycle is the starting place for diagnosing your condition. Are you a quad I, II, III, or IV church? What leadership challenges are you facing? What skills must you learn to navigate through these phases?

The Key Indicators

Here is another way to think about this. Congregations have four indicators to measure health: energy, inclusion, programs, and administration. At each stage in the life of a church, these indicators play a more or less active role. These roles are indicated by the upper and lower case letters on the graph.

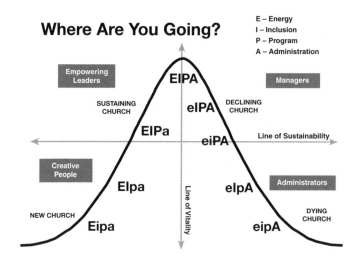

The "Energy" indicator highlights the level at which the congregation is motivated into action around the vision and mission of the church. It speaks to the spirit of the faith community as well as its passion about its ministries. The "Inclusion" indicator highlights the dedication and enthusiasm of church participants to invite people to be a part of the ministries of the church. It speaks to an outward focus on growth and an intentional commitment to hospitality. The "Program" indicator highlights the level at which the church is able to start, grow, and maintain ministries that transform both the community and the people within the church. These are particular to each church context and to the needs of the people within the church. The final indicator, "Administration," highlights the need of every church to have systems that promote growth through policies, procedures, and staffing. Collectively, these indicators tell a story of where a church might be in its lifecycle.[2]

A New Framework

I had just finished reviewing this framework with a group of lay leaders in a congregation in Los Angeles when an older man in the back raised his hand. "I don't disagree with anything that you have said here," he said, "but life is never this simple. We are missing deeper insights because we are ignoring the mess. Sometimes new patterns emerge from what looks like chaos." I felt a tightening of my chest, and a deep resonance in my gut. "Yes!" my body whispered. The bell curve has its place in our learning, but it's insufficient on its own to talk about the emerging patterns of our modern life.

Shortly after this conversation, on August 9, 2014, news reports filled our televisions screens about Michael Brown, a young unarmed African American man, being shot and killed by Darren Wilson, a 28-year-old white police officer in St. Louis, Missouri. People of good conscience across the nation stood paralyzed watching Michael Brown's body lying face down in the street as the news reports kept playing the story. Seeing Michael Brown's dead body reinforced what many of us feared to be true about our enforcement systems – our police were killing unarmed black people. The shooting sparked huge protests with thousands of people descending upon the city, marching in the streets. Michael Brown's killing certainly wasn't the first unjust murder of a young black man, but it became the tipping point for the #BlackLivesMatter movement.

Two years before Michael Brown's death, 20-year-old Adam Lanza, killed twenty-six people and himself in what became known as the Sandy Hook Elementary school shooting in Newtown, Connecticut. He first killed his mother at their shared home before taking her guns and driving to the school. Lanza brought four guns with him. He killed twenty first-grade children aged six and seven during the attack at school, along with six adults, including four teachers, the principal, and the school psychologist. Lanza then killed himself as police arrived at the school. We as a nation didn't know what to make of this; he had killed children…so many children. At the Prayer Vigil on December 16, 2012, President Barack Obama reminded us of our responsibility:

> *Can we honestly say that we're doing enough to keep our children—all of them—safe from harm? Can we claim, as a nation, that we're all together there, letting them know they are loved and teaching them to love in return? Can we say that we're truly doing enough to give all the children of this country the chance they deserve to live out their lives in happiness and with purpose?*

I've been reflecting on this the last few days, and if we're honest with ourselves, the answer is no. We're not doing enough. And we will have to change.

Since I've been President, this is the fourth time we have come together to comfort a grieving community torn apart by a mass shooting. The fourth time we've hugged survivors. The fourth time we've consoled the families of victims. And in between, there have been an endless series of deadly shootings across the country, almost daily reports of victims, many of them children, in small towns and in big cities all across America—victims whose—much of the time, their only fault was being at the wrong place at the wrong time.

We can't tolerate this anymore. These tragedies must end. And to end them, we must change. We will be told that the causes of such violence are complex, and that is true. No single law—no set of laws can eliminate evil from the world, or prevent every senseless act of violence in our society.

But that can't be an excuse for inaction. Surely, we can do better than this.[3]

The debates for gun control legislation gained speed but went nowhere. On October 24, 2014, 15-year-old freshman, Jaylen Fryberg, shot five students in the school cafeteria of Marysville Pilchuck High School, fatally wounding four, before committing suicide. Fifty-nine more school shootings took place around the country before February 14, 2018, when 19-year-old former student, Nikolas Cruz, began shooting students and staff members with a semi-automatic AR-15 type rifle at Marjory Stoneman Douglas High School in Clearwater, Florida, after activating a fire alarm. Seventeen people were killed, and 17 others were injured.[4] The madness was too much. Once again, thousands took to the streets in protest as part of the #MarchForOurLives movement.

We live in an age of movements made notable by the hashtags that power their viral spread online. Let's remember just a few of the ones we have seen between 2015 and 2018:[5]

- #NotOneMore
- #LoveWins
- #WomensMarch
- #BringBackOurGirls
- #StandwithPP
- #Health4All

- #DressLikeAWoman

- #DefendDACA

- #FamiliesBelongTogether

- #MeToo

- #TakeAKnee

- #EqualPay

Each one of these represents a mobilization of masses of people making new demands of the norms and institutions that have structured our world for the past 100 years. It's as if minority and marginalized groups are rising up day after day, month after month, year after year to say, "The way things are working isn't working for me and my family. It's time for our social contract, our institutions, and our laws to change."

Movements are sparked by a triggering event—a shooting, a victim standing up for her rights, a mother desperately trying to protect her child while seeking asylum at our border. Whatever the triggering event, it sparks a surge of activism—protests, media coverage, lawmakers pledging changes. But change is hard to create and sustain, and the masses soon move on or become disillusioned by the slow progress. Knowing we can't give up, we assess our strategies based on what we have learned and design an action plan possible over months or years of strategic pressure against the institutions we are seeking to change. In this way we become a more focused, more developed, and more mature force, capable of establishing the change we seek. The Movement NetLab[6] generated a helpful image to illustrate the pattern:

The Movement Cycle

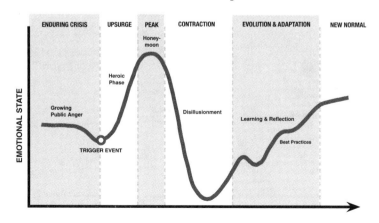

As I studied this model, I felt a sense of familiarity, as if I have lived this journey personally and walked with congregations through the same. Then, I turned it upside down.

Our Heroic Journey

If you are a Jungian analyst or a follower of Joseph Campbell, you will recognize this pattern as the "Hero's Journey," the archetypal journey of a common person called to a grand adventure, completing a transformational task, and then returning to his/her community as a more mature and deeply developed person. We see echoes of this archetypal journey when Jesus went away into the desert for 40 days, conquered the temptations put before him by the devil, and then returned to his community ready to begin his ministry. We tell similar stories of Moses and the Israelites, of the Buddha, and of Mohammed.

Could it be that, just as you as an individual go on your own heroic quest, your church also has its own call to a transformational heroic journey? What if we are not living in days of decline, but are being invited on a wild and unpredictable heroic journey toward a more mature and developed expression of faith? If that is the case, I have good news for us. We know the contours of this journey; we have been on it for thousands of years. We don't know the specific obstacles that may come our way, but we know the journey ends with resurrection and new life.

What does that look like in practical terms? If we consider the Hero's Journey, we can see how a congregation might navigate change and conflict, embrace hope, and mature as an organizational culture.

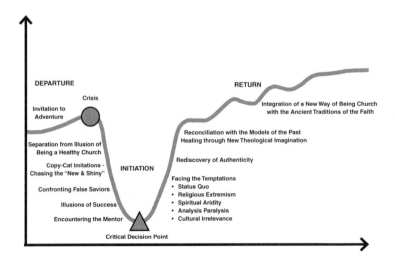

Consider the journey in three phases: departure, initiation, and return. Think of a time when your congregation was invited into a new challenge. Rev. Alison Harrington, pastor of Southside Presbyterian Church in Tucson, Arizona, remembers in 2016 when Daniel Neyoy Ruiz, an undocumented immigrant who was facing a deportation order after a routine traffic stop, approached her church with his lawyer asking for sanctuary. Alison called her leaders together, and they prayed about what they should do. They talked to others about what might be involved. They had to consider liability issues. They wondered if they could sustain the daily demands housing a family would make on their community. They feared that people in their community who disagreed with their stance might physically threaten them. But they knew they were being called to a higher mission. They talked, prayed, and listened. Then, they said, "Yes."

After living at the church with his wife and American-born son for a month, Neyoy Ruiz was granted a stay in his case. Saying "yes" to this adventure positioned the church as a national leader in the Sanctuary Movement, which has seen a resurgence since 2016. They have become a guide and mentor to hundreds of other congregations across the nation, having gained a depth of knowledge, perspective, and wisdom from having walked this treacherous road. Rev. Harrington says, "I've learned that sanctuary is not just about taking residence within [the] walls [of a church];...it's about finding...shelter and protection within a community."[7]

The beginning of the heroic journey is both exciting and disorienting. You will meet mentors—other congregations or individual pastors or coaches—along the way who have a sense of your next best steps. Often in our consulting work, we are called into congregations as they are just beginning this phase. They are looking for a guide to walk with them. Ironically, most congregations come to us asking for help with a strategic plan. They want to plan their transformation. I explain that, while planning is fine, this kind of journey doesn't follow a map. We *sense* our way to our "next best step," iterating as we go. Navigating requires an intuition and a spiritual fitness that grows over time, with each phase.

Inevitably, on any grand adventure you face challenges that demand more than you think you can give. They test your resolve and your commitment. They challenge your understanding of yourself—the core of who you believe you are. As your progress through the Initiation Phase, you can expect a pattern: You face the reality that you aren't the healthy congregation you thought you were. You might hit a conflict or crisis in the church that causes people to leave, or discover that you will be out of cash in a couple of years. Something happens to shatter your illusion of safety and sustainability.

With this new realization, you may look for quick solutions. You think, "Buying that new stewardship program will solve the problem!" or, "If we just sang praise music, more families with kids would come." You survey other churches that are growing and copy what they are doing. You spend critical time and energy looking for the path of least resistance and fastest fix. You come up empty-handed.

Once you realize that easy solutions are not going to solve your problems, you start looking for more disruptive changes. "The church is in trouble," you think, "so it must be the pastor's fault. Let's fire this one and get a new guy in here." You start looking for saviors, and people step up with the perfect church renewal solutions that never quite deliver the perfect church renewal results. Again, you are lost.

As you spend more time in this space, you meet people who have genuine wisdom and understand the life-death-life journey. They have a spiritual maturity that gives them eyes to see a longer trajectory and strategic options for your congregation. Sometimes these people are consultants or denominational leaders. Sometimes they are members or community leaders. You will recognize them because they know the contours of this road, having walked it before.

With your mentor or guide in place, you reach your critical decision point. Do you face the challenges ahead, or do you abandon the challenge, inevitably leading to death? Many churches complete assessment programs, paying hundreds of dollars for diagnosis of their context and condition, only to do nothing in response. They fail to make any decisions at all about their future—which is a decision in itself.

Should you accept the challenge, you are accepting the hard work of facing the common temptations of congregational decline:

- **Defaulting Back to the Status Quo:** It will be easy in the days ahead to default back to the equilibrium state of "the way it's always been." Systems produce what they are designed to produce, and you are taking on the challenge of changing the system in such fundamental ways that it changes its projected future (what it produces). You have to sustain the changes you institute with a relentless rigor, and you have to do it together.

- **Religious Extremism:** When congregations are in transitional phases, a group of people may rise up to say, "If we were more biblical and more disciplined in our faith, we wouldn't be having these problems. We are struggling because God is punishing our unfaithfulness." This nativist message has its actual roots in historic patriarchy and the "strong man" or "angry father" archetype that says, "We need command, order, and discipline to be strong." Individuals raised in that kind of environment as children are particularly vulnerable to this message. It provides them the comfort of knowing where they fit in the chain of command. Religious extremism can't survive without this top-down power structure and the fear-based message that if we don't get things under control all will be lost. Don't fall for it.

- **Spiritual Aridity:** The flip side of spiritual extremism is spiritual aridity, in which you may become deeply agnostic about the value of your spiritual heritage and theological foundation. Your understanding of faith can becomes more of an intellectual exercise than a lived experience. You may not be at all certain that the Christian faith makes the world a better place, and, if pushed, might abandon it in favor of a more generic humanistic view. The practices of faith—prayer, devotions, fasting, worship—don't feed you the way they once did. At first, you wondered what was wrong with you, but now you wonder what's relevant about these practices.

- **Analysis Paralysis:** Mainline congregations are particularly good at researching *ad nauseam.* They love to complete surveys and demographic research. The more graphs, charts, and spreadsheets one can have, the better. Many congregations gets stuck in this phase, as if additional information would finally reveal the perfect solution. They never take the steps to implement anything they learn through the research. They stay paralyzed until they declined to such a point that decisions are made for them by their financial collapse.

- **Cultural Irrelevance:** It is possible to gather every single week in a church building, sing songs, say prayers, and listen to sermons, and then have absolutely no impact on the world. It's possible to attend church or live an entire life and never connect social action with contemplation. Jesus didn't just disappear into the wilderness indefinitely; he went to there to be refreshed and then return to the world to be of service. It will be tempting to hide because you're either overwhelmed by the needs of your community or you have no imagination concerning how your congregation can make a difference. You have to face this temptation head-on because it's at the heart of your theological calling and power.

You may meet other temptations along the way that test the very soul of your congregation. Face them head-on, and after each one you will rediscover the original dream that founded your church and the deep, life-giving authenticity that will carry it forward. You become *real* in this journey, like the old rocking horse explains in the children's book, *The Velveteen Rabbit.*

The final step in the journey is that of reconciliation and return. The journey has changed you. You've found your space of authenticity. You've learned about what drives you, what you stand for. You know you are capable of far more than you dreamed or imagined. You also know your weaknesses and blind spots. You're honest about your vulnerabilities. Your transformation is both visible and contagious—and, now, you are ready to walk with others on their own heroic journeys.

In the process of the return, you will reconcile yourself to the "in-between-ness" of this age in which church structures must be reimagined with more theological integrity. We need models of church that abandon patriarchal power as their organizing assumption. We need models that expose the inherent racism of our mainline systems. We need models that care more about spiritual formation than salary structures. The pressure to maintain what we have is enormous. The journey for your congregation is to live between these worlds, a bridge between what is and what is to come.

My friend and colleague, Brian McLaren, has often talked about congregations as being "Schools of Love." They are the places we go to become more loving people. They are the places where we love one another so genuinely as we traverse these heroic journeys as a congregation and as individuals that, through the experience, we finally return to our true selves. That is the gift of being a part of a congregation on a journey. We are a "People of the Way," on an adventure to bring more love, kindness, and compassion into our world. I can't imagine anything more fundamental to our flight as people than that.

A Personal Practice: Your Manifesto

A personal manifesto is an expression of your core values, beliefs, and priorities. It represents what you stand for and how you intend to live your life. It is both descriptive of who you are and prescriptive of how you wish to act in the world. Today, you are going to write your personal manifesto. I would start with a pad of Post-It Notes because I love them. You can also just write these on a pad of paper.

1. Start by **writing down your core values.** What values define how you want to live your life and make decisions? Kindness? Integrity? Ingenuity? Courage? Patience? Honesty? Bravery?

2. Next, **write a list of strengths** you observe in yourself. We always want to play to our strengths. Are you a good listener? Are you a visionary? Are you detail-oriented? Work well on a team? Good at managing people?

3. Now **write down your passions.** Do you want to build clean water wells in Africa? Are you passionate about stopping human trafficking? Do you care about opioid usage in your community?

4. Next, **write down what keeps you up at night.** What breaks your heart? What makes you want to rise up in action and change it? What can't you accept in the world?

5. Now **write down what life experiences have shaped you**. What failures have made you stronger? What successes helped you grow? What have you learned in your relationships that taught you about yourself?

You will have a bunch of used Post-It Notes at this point. Start to notice themes in them that can serve as headers or headlines for your manifesto. Once you see four to six headlines, write out one paragraph below each one that expands on what you mean. Here is an example from *my* personal manifesto you might use as a guide for yours:

My Personal Manifesto
By Rev. Cameron Trimble

I am brave and kind.

I need to be both. I am fierce in the face of injustice and oppression. I lean in. I want to know success and prosperity. I aim to embrace all that my life can manifest. And I want to be known for my kindness towards people and our planet. I am both warrior and protector, creator and team player. My kindness should never be confused with weakness. Sometimes kindness feels painful. Kindness is always grounded in the best intentions for the other, sometimes at great cost to yourself.

I am connected to you.

We belong to one another. We are each other's keepers. I aim to show up as the fullest and most authentic expression of myself in my life with others. I strive to make my leadership an expression of my courage, my vulnerability, and my commitment to make a difference. I am in the game for all of us. I embrace our interdependence.

Stories matter.

I care about the stories we tell ourselves and each other about our possibilities and our constraints. I am committed to authoring stories of empowerment and hope. I also learn from our *cantadoras*, our tellers of the ancient stories, because I believe our deepest collective wisdom is held in the stories of our ancestors—past, present, and future. These stories help us find our Way. I listen closely to them and cherish the ways they teach us and heal us.

Adventure calls to me.

I love to feel alive. I propel myself into adventures. I am a pilot. I am a pastor. I am a world traveler. I am a hiker. I am a horse rider. I am an author. I am a national speaker. I am a whitewater rafter. I am a "Crossfitter." I am a leader. I am a daughter. I am a mother. I am a sister...and I long to be so much more. I become these things, and they become a part of me. They become the sources of my inspiration and teachers of a life well-lived.

Once you have finished your own personal manifesto, put it in a place you will see it every day. Mine sits on my desk. I look at it daily as a reminder of who I am and who I am committed to be.

A Congregational Practice: A Congregational Manifesto

Let's create a manifesto for your congregation using a similar process to the personal manifest.

1. Start by **writing down your congregation's core values.** What are the values that define how you want to live together and make decisions? Kindness? Integrity? Ingenuity? Courage? Patience? Honesty? Bravery?

2. Next, **write a list of strengths** you observe in your church. Think about the moments in your history that make you the most proud. Have you taken courageous stands for justice? Have you taken on a major challenge in your community and made a difference?

3. Now **write down your passions.** What ministries rally the most people? Which have endured the longest?

4. Next, **write down what concerns you, as a congregation, have for your community.?** What breaks your heart? What makes you want to rise up in action and change it? What can't you accept in the world?

5. Now **write down what shared experiences have shaped you.** Think about times you came together and did something great. Think of times when a death in the congregation shook you to the core. Think of times of conflict. What failures have made you stronger? Think of the generations who have attended and where they are now because of the church. Think of the staff members who inspired you to dream new dreams for your church.

Start to group these into themes. Just like above, create short statements that you then develop into a single paragraph. Or, you might write out a poem. Or, you can create a statement. Here is an example from a church that I love, called Highlands Church in Denver, Colorado:

Married, divorced and single here, it's one family that mingles here.

Conservative and liberal here, we've all gotta give a little here.

Big and small here, there's room for us all here.

Doubt and believe here, we all can receive here.

LGBTQ and straight here, there's no hate here.

Woman and man here, everyone can here.

Whatever your race here, for all of us grace here.

In imitation of the ridiculous love Almighty God has for each of us and all of us,

let us live and love without labels!

This is both aspirational and inspirational. It speaks to who they are and who they want to be. It's also memorable.

The format of your manifesto is entirely up to you. What matters is that you take the time to create it. Good luck.

Small Group Discussion Questions

1. Where do you think your congregation is on the bell curve lifecycle? Are you in a phase of growth or decline? Are you above the line of financial sustainability or below it?

2. How would you tell the heroic journey of your congregation? Tell the story...

3. What national movements does your church support? How has being involved changed your congregation?

4. What could your church do in the next six months to improve the quality of life for the people in your community? What is your next best step?

---

[1]To read more about the congregational lifecycle, reference Michael Piazza and Cameron Trimble, *Liberating Hope: Daring to Renew the Mainline Church* (Cleveland: Pilgrim Press, 2011).

[2]To read more about the congregational lifecycle, reference Michael Piazza and Cameron Trimble, *Liberating Hope: Daring to Renew the Mainline Church* (Cleveland: Pilgrim Press, 2011).

[3]https://obamawhitehouse.archives.gov/blog/2012/12/16/president-obama-prayer -vigil-connecticut-shooting-victims-newtown-you-are-not-alone

[4]https://en.wikipedia.org/wiki/List_of_school_shootings_in_the_United_States#2015_to_present

[5]https://www.globalcitizen.org/en/content/hashtag-activism-hashtag 10-twitter-trends-dresslik/

[6] https://ussen.org/portfolio/movement-cycle-worksheet/

[7] https://www.youtube.com/watch?v=lvOEM8IaZgU

Chapter Four

Your Flight Crew

Checklist

- ❑ Complete flight team orientation for the specific plane, your expectations as captain, and the details of the flight plan

- ❑ Engage in pre-flight team-building so that people feel they know each other a bit

- ❑ Assign roles and responsibilities for the flight

- ❑ Pray no one is crazy

"The most effective way to do it is to do it."
—Amelia Earhart, first woman to fly across the Atlantic Ocean

Like most newbies wanting to learn to fly, I spent hours researching flight schools, their teaching philosophies, their aircraft fleet, their maintenance records, their reputation at the airfield... I'm kidding. Actually, I chose my flight school because they had the best-looking website. I'm serious.

Sometimes, you don't know where to start. So, you start where you can. I am sure there were better and more sophisticated ways to find a flight school. If I were to start looking again today, I would have some different questions to ask. But ultimately, even after the best due diligence, you simply have to take a step to call and say, "Hi, I'm Cameron and I want to learn how to fly." You pray someone on the other end of the line knows what to do with that confession.

I got lucky. When I walked into my flight school for the first time, I met the wonderful man who would become my personal flight instructor. Jim had been a certified flight instructor for two years and had taught dozens of students. His goal was to become a commercial airline pilot (which he is today) and he was…wait for it…*twenty-three* years old. In even better news, he was one of the best pilots I could imagine.

Jim had logged over 1,000 hours of "pilot in command" flight time on his way toward becoming certified as a commercial airline pilot by the time we started working together. He was teaching at my flight school because that is generally the only way pilots who are not in the military can fly enough to qualify for commercial flight. If any of us are lucky enough to fly with Jim when we board our commercial planes, we can rest assured we are with one of the most highly skilled and disciplined pilots I can imagine. Jim is the real deal.

What wasn't guaranteed was that Jim would be a great fit for me. For us to be effective in this partnership, Jim and I needed to be in complete synchronicity. We needed to be a team.

In churches, you are never a solo operator. You are required to work with many and diverse groups of people, some of whom seem to attend just to work out their childhood traumas on you. You have to be adept at forming, building, and mobilizing effective teams. In fact, developing an effective team is the most important thing you will ever do. Here is why: churches do not grow larger than their leader's capacity.

Why Your Team Matters

The average-size church in America today has about 75 members. Why is that? As it turns out, 75 people is about all one leader can manage effectively before either the leader or the system collapses. Mind you, collapse isn't the only possible outcome. If you are a good leader, you know the power of building teams of people to help you. You know that the best use of your time is not *doing* the ministry for others, but *investing* in the leadership development of new leaders who can do the ministry at a larger (or simply healthier) scale.

Of course, your challenge is that you have about eight million "most important things" on your leadership to-do list. If you are the pastor, you are expected to preach great sermons, be present at every meeting; network with every community group; visit every person in the hospital; baptize, marry, and bury people; lead small groups and Bible studies; be the most visionary prophet in the land… Lord, I am tired just writing this. If you are the stalwart lay leader, your job is to serve on every committee (for thirty years in a row), attend every service, spend at least twenty hours a week at the church, and teach Sunday school. Forget having a personal life.

Here is the thing: actually, none of this is your job. Your job is not to be the saint of the church, working yourself to death in the service of your congregation. Your job is to *equip* the saints. Let me say that again: your job as a leader is to make sure that you equip *others* to be the ministers of the church. Ephesians 4:11–13 reminds us: "The gifts [God] gave were that some would be apostles, some prophets, some evangelists, some pastors and teachers, to *equip the saints* for the work of ministry, for building up the body of Christ, until all of us come to the unity of the faith and of the knowledge of the Son of God, to maturity, to the measure of the full stature of Christ" (NRSV, emphasis added). You are not called to burn out, over-function, or justify your existence by making yourself invaluable to your congregation. Actually, your calling is the opposite. The greatest gift you give a church is building teams that enable ministry to flourish without the sacrifice or suffering of individuals.

Flying has been a good teacher for me. There are two moments in a typical flight that can easily overwhelm a solo pilot. The first is at taxi, take-off, and climb, when you are talking with ground control and then the tower to get clearance to take off. You have to listen to their commands, repeat them back, change frequencies, get the plane onto the runway quickly and take off, full throttle into the wind while aiming for the perfect climb slope. If you pull your nose too high, you risk a stall; pull your nose down and you risk failing to clear obstacles at the end of the runway, such as that line of trees and the radio tower that just appeared out of nowhere.

The second moment for "overwhelmation" is in landing. You are 15 miles out approaching the airport. You need to get the weather report on ATIS while also monitoring the traffic control frequency. You write down the wind direction, temperature, dew point, your new altimeter settings, active runways, and any other pertinent NOTAM (Notice to Airmen) information. You make your call to the tower:

> **You:** "Peachtree tower, Skyhawk 1097Y, 10 miles to the northeast, inbound for full stop with information Bravo."
>
> **Tower:** "Roger, 1097Y, notify when 4 miles out and ident. Inbound for runway 3R, traffic at 3 o'clock headed northeast."
>
> **You:** "Notify 4 miles out, ident, inbound for 3R, looking for traffic, 1097Y."

I know what you are thinking: What is the big deal? Just repeat everything back to them and fly the plane. But while you are communicating with ATC, you also need to be pressing the IDENT button on your transponder so that they can track your approach, maintaining your course direction and altitude, looking for the traffic they just alerted you to, pulling up the airport map on your iPad, getting the ground control frequency programmed into your comms radio and planning your approach into the airport.

These are the moments that make or break good teams. You have to recognize that you can't—you shouldn't—do it all, and that you need to be clear from the beginning about who is in charge of what. When flying with another pilot, we always split the workload. I handle the comms and fly the plane. My copilot keeps their eyes out for the oncoming plane and pulls up the map to double-check my approach strategy. The key is that we discuss this before we ever leave the ground. We know team work is essential to our success, and we take the steps to ensure that we work seamlessly together.

A Strong Team Starts with You

I am sitting on a Delta flight going from Sacramento to Atlanta. The flight attendants have closed the boarding door at the gate and completed their safety brief, in which they remind us that, in the event of an emergency, we are to put on our own oxygen masks before helping others. That makes sense, of course, because you can't help others if you are running out of oxygen yourself.

Can I state the obvious to you? You can't do it all yourself. I watch so many pastors and committed lay leaders try. It's like they can't say "no." They have no filter for saying "enough." Then they burn out. Or they screw up. Or they self-sabotage. People get hurt. It's never pretty. So, let me say it again in case you are on the cusp of joining the ranks of the over-functioning leaders with savior complexes: you can't do effective ministry by yourself—and you shouldn't even try. So, don't.

Beyond trying to save the world, you are well-served by knowing your strengths and weaknesses. Church planting pastor Dale Galloway, is credited with saying that a true leader is not someone who can do the work of ten people, but someone who can organize ten people to do the work. I am a fan of the Enneagram, StrengthsFinder, and other personality assessment tools that help you gain a better sense of your gifts and areas for growth. When you are aware of these, you can build teams of people who have gifts you might not possess.

It took me a long time to learn this lesson. When I first started in ministry, I almost ran a youth ministry program into the ground. I was at the church morning, noon, and night designing all of the programming and buying or creating all of the supplies for our games and activities. I even learned to play the guitar so that I, and I alone, could lead the group in music. As it turns out, I can't sing. It also turns out that I'm not particularly "crafty," so any props I created for our games or activities would have qualified for the Etsy "Fail" page of their website. No one could help me, though many tried. In the end, my lack of self-awareness did three things: it robbed other leaders of the chance to contribute; it robbed the youth of a more creative experience; and, while it certainly fed my ego, it wore me out. Learn from my mistake.

The Leader's Job Is to Be Clear

When you ask some leaders how they build their teams, they will say things such as, "I hire the right people, and get out of the way." That is never true. You can't just bring people onto a team and not provide inspiration, direction, and feedback. It doesn't matter how brilliant a person may be, if they don't know where you are going, how you plan to get there, what their responsibilities are for helping, and how they will be held accountable, they won't perform at their top level. Your job is to be clear about the vision, mission, strategies, goals, and expected outcomes. If you aren't clear, no one else will be either.

Most churches get in trouble here. We write fancy, carefully worded mission statements that no one can remember. We include everyone's pet projects in our ministry structures. We write annual work plans that grow and grow until we have 15 critical priorities. We are stretched painfully thin and ask our team to join us in that madness. Jim Collins, the author of the best-selling management books *Good to Great* and *Built to Last,* is quoted as saying: "If you have more than three priorities, you don't have any."[1]

As the leader, your job is to be clear about where you are going, how you are getting there, who is in charge of what along the way, and how people will be held accountable to their commitments. Can you imagine boarding a flight, and the captain comes over the intercom to say, "Good morning, ladies and gentlemen, welcome aboard! We know that you thought you were boarding the plane flying from Atlanta to Miami, but the first officer and I are debating whether Chicago might be a better destination. It's so pretty there this time of year. We aren't sure about our fuel burn, so we may have to stop along the way for refueling. There have to be airports big enough for us to pop in for some fuel. We will work it out and let you know. For now, sit back, relax, and enjoy the flight." I'm afraid that the invitation we offer to new participants coming to our churches sounds a bit like this. We say, "Welcome! We have no idea how we are living out the Ways of Jesus around here or why we have most of the programs we do, but we hope you enjoy hanging out with us. We are nice people and want to make you feel really welcome. Oh, and do you have young children by chance? We need more of those around here."

At Virginia Highland Church, a congregation that I copastored for four years in Atlanta, Georgia, we used Micah 6:8 as our vision and mission frame. We plastered that scripture everywhere:

"What does the Lᴏʀᴅ require of you
but to do justice, and to love kindness,
and to walk humbly with your God?"

Doing Justice, Loving Kindness, and Walking Humbly became the three lenses through which we acted in the world and structured our teams and ministries. We believed the balance of these three commands in someone's life helped them become a little more like Jesus...which is, after all, the point of all of this. "Doing Justice" became the frame for our community activism work. "Loving Kindness" served as the frame for our congregational care ministries. "Walking Humbly" directed our spiritual formation, small groups, and personal development programs. Our Sunday worship experiences included an emphasis on all three areas. When you joined the church, you were expected to be a participant in all three areas, because the balance shapes us more completely. We were clear as a congregation about our values, our ways of being in the world, and the difference we wanted to make in the city.

What frame could you put in place for your leaders that is memorable, clear, comprehensive and makes a difference? It could be a scripture, as we used at Virginia Highland Church. It could be a baseball diamond, as Rick Warren used at Saddleback Church. It could be three powerful words. It could be a statement. Whatever you choose, make sure it resonates with your congregation so that they know where you all are going together, and where they fit in that journey.

Recruiting Your Ace Flight Team

The best advice my leadership coach ever gave me was simple: "Find people smarter than you, and recruit them to your team." You quickly discover that a diverse team is far more effective than one that looks, acts, talks, and walks just as you do. You don't want a team that acquiesces to you. To adapt to our rapidly changing world, you need the creativity, divergent thinking, and ingenuity that comes with a dynamic team as you lead your congregation or ministry area into its most powerful expression.

Do you remember that iconic scene in the movie *Apollo 13*? In a routine step on their daily checklist, the crew refreshed the oxygen canisters. That refresh caused an electrical overload that sparked a fire, forcing them to shut down the oxygen system. As it turns out, that same system also powered the three fuel cells that provided power to the command ship's instruments. Realizing the problem, Jim Lovell and his crew didn't try to solve the problem themselves. They immediately radioed to engineers and technicians at Mission Control in the Kennedy Space Center and explained what was going on. Mission Control pulled every brilliant mind they had on the team to work on a solution. No one person could have solved it alone. They needed the diverse team of engineers, flight dynamics specialists, scientists, electricians, mission director, and medical personnel to get those astronauts safely back to earth.

You need that kind of team too. Imagine working with a group of people where everyone is in it together, in which each person's contribution is unique, makes a difference, and, without it, your mission would fail. A friend of mine, a woman who is both brilliant and strategic in her leadership, recently started a new job leading one of our nation's premiere religious organizations. She inherited a staff and a structure that needed reinvention to ensure its future remained strong. On her first official day with her new team, she sent out an email to the entire organization establishing her expectations for the kind of culture they would create among themselves. Included in the letter was a powerful vision about what it means to work as a healthy team:

> *Perhaps some thoughts about my expectations and style would be helpful. I expect us to maintain a professional environment both in the office and when we are out in the world representing [this organization]. We are a service organization and should approach our work with a service disposition. I am direct and honest and expect the same from you. I sometimes make mistakes. I expect all of us to make mistakes sometimes. I will not hide my mistakes from you, and you should not hide your mistakes from me. I value questions. I will ask questions and I want you to ask questions. Questions help us produce better outcomes. Questions help us realize that no one has all the answers. I expect us all to practice generous listening. Generous listening has two aspects: (1) the listener assumes the good intentions of the speaker, and (2) the listener listens to hear as opposed to listening with a view toward responding. We should always try to be aware of our own (individual and institutional) underlying presuppositions—and make them explicit whenever possible. I expect us to brainstorm, to create spaces for innovation, to be willing to try new ideas.*
>
> *I expect us to view professional criticism as healthy. I appreciate Sanjeev Himachali's perspective: "Criticism is part of learning and growth. It means that you are taking initiatives to learn something new and grow over from your current state. If you are not getting criticized, it means you are not taking enough risk to learn something new and to grow." I am happy to talk with you about ways to receive, and offer, criticism.*
>
> *In my view, we all have skill sets. None of us has all skill sets necessary to meet our mission.*

She understood that if they wanted to be a leading organization in their field, they needed everyone on their team to show up with 100 percent of their best talent, energy, and focus. They couldn't accomplish what they were committed to in their mission without each person on the team bringing their "A" game and trusting that it would be honored and amplified by their teammates. She also knew something else: your best team leaders want to be on a team with high expectations in place. They want to play with the pros. By establishing a culture of excellence, she was creating the context to attract the best.

Let Them Fly

I walked into a huge banquet hall after a long day of inspiring sessions at the MAKERS Conference. Each year, this conference gathers the best and brightest across many industry sectors for networking, inspiration, and collaborative strategy building. You have to be invited to attend, and you never know who you might run into while you are there. I stood in the doorway staring at the sea of tables prepped for our dinner session. No assigned seats, so I chose one close to the stage. I sat down and turned to my left, beginning the expected process of introducing myself to my tablemates. I extended my hand and then looked into the face of the man to my left. "No freaking way," I whispered. I was staring into the face of NASA Astronaut Leland Melvin smiling back at me. Trying to be cool, I immediately told him in a single breath that he was one of my heroes and I was a pilot and I couldn't believe I was meeting him and I wanted to know everything he knew about flying and space and engineering and *ALL THE THINGS*. He laughed. I blushed. Then for the thirty minutes he humored me with amazing stories.

"Here is how they taught me to fly in NASA," he said. "They put me into a T-38 fighter jet at night and had me fly across the country with almost no help from the other pilot in the plane. I had to handle flying, navigation, comms, everything." As he was talking, I laughed, remembering my first flight. He went on, "After you freak out, then you settle in and figure it out. It was actually a really good way to learn." He's right. He wasn't up there alone; had he gotten into trouble, an experienced pilot was there to help. But he was given as much freedom as possible in a focused, controlled environment to learn two key lessons: first, how to fly a fighter jet by instinct; and, second, what it felt like to push through the fear and keep leading. That night, he learned another lesson in discovering what he was made of.

If your core team members are strong, they will thrive in an environment in which they have the freedom to experiment, take risks, fail, succeed, learn, and advance your shared mission. The best gift you can give them as the team lead is to *let them fly*. Give them the support that they need—clarity about the destination, the resources at their disposal, what to do if they need help—and then let them go. You are creating a permission-giving culture that not only attracts the best leaders but also develops the most generative ministries.

Celebrate the Wins

When we first started the Center for Progressive Renewal, now over ten years ago, we had a motto that we used in our team: "Committed to Excellence; Focused on Fun." We were a start-up organization tasked with developing programs that supported people starting new churches or renewing existing ones. As with all new organizations, we had really good days when we knew that our work was making a difference. We also had really bad days when we discovered that we had dropped the ball or a client wasn't pleased. The emotional rollercoaster of the early days of a new venture aren't for the faint of heart. But we decided early in our launch that we would celebrate our wins.

Celebrating the wins (the good days, the good programs, the good work our clients were achieving) became critical as a way to register our accomplishments and remind us of how far we had come. It's easy to keep working day after day and fail to see the difference you are making. We had a little brass bell in our office that we would ring every time someone called us with a story of success from their church. Everyone in the office would cheer. When we worked out an agreement with a new denominational partner, we would add their name on a printed piece of paper to our "Wall of World-Changing Wonders" so that we saw their name every day and remembered that we were in this together to make a difference for their churches. When we launched a new program and it wasn't a total fail, we went out to dinner as a staff team to celebrate.

We could have just as easily focused on everything that wasn't going well. God knows we had plenty of that too. Focusing on the wins inspired us to keep trying, keep innovating, keep calling, keep dreaming, keep believing, keep producing, keep coaching, keep hoping. It kept us in the game, with each other, knowing that while we weren't perfect, we could see that our contribution to the wider church was making an impact.

Your congregation or ministry team may have a hard time seeing the difference they are making in the church and the community. Your job is to remind them. In a sense, you need only hold up a mirror and show them *who they already are* and *what they are already doing* that makes the world a more just and generous place. This had a multiplying effect. When they see the "wins" they make possible for others, they will want to do more.

So, celebrate all the time. Celebrate the wins during your worship service, in your newsletters, on your website, in your staff/council meetings, in your small group gatherings, and in your ministry committee meetings. Make the people in the congregation doing such great work the heroes of the church instead of just your elected leaders. They are the ones creating the "wins" for the beloved community, and it's their actions that you want to multiply. Celebrate their vision, tenacity, kindness and courage. Remember: what you feed, grows.

Debrief Together

Regardless of the outcome of an experiment or experience, you want to bring your teams together to debrief. This accomplishes two things: first, it reminds everyone that we are in this together, so you are not alone. Second, it creates a culture of accountable learning that helps you see new possibilities, patterns, and connections.

An exercise I use often in my work with churches involves asking a team in a debrief session to divide into groups of three people. I then ask them to debrief the experience as if they were consultants working with the team on the project. This invites them to place themselves outside of the experience itself as objective observers. I ask them to consider the following questions:

1. What conditions existed that generated the outcome that they saw?

2. What could have been added, changed, or removed that would have improved the outcome?

3. Did they accomplish what they set out to accomplish?

4. How could they have worked in even greater alignment as a team?

These four questions help clarify the conditions of the experiment, what improvements might be possible to the conditions and the team, and if the experiment in this iteration was ultimately successful.

What should you debrief? *Everything.* Debrief your Sunday services. Debrief your youth group activities. Debrief your council/vestry/consistory meetings. Debrief your staff meetings. Debrief your choir rehearsals. Debrief your congregational meetings. Debrief your newsletters. Debrief your mission trips. Debrief everything as much as possible. You will build a currency of trust between your members that becomes invaluable as you continue to try new things in the life of the congregation.

The Trust Factor

Let me say a word about trust: All teams work at the speed of trust. If trust is missing, your team won't function. If trust is limited, your team will hold back. If trust is free-flowing, your team will excel.

In his book, *The Five Dysfunctions of a Team,* Patrick Lencioni notes that trust is both given (offered without evidence it will be honored) and generated (earned over time).[2] When we are new to a team or committee, we gift our team with our trust. We don't have a history established to know if our trust is a good investment or not. We have to offer it freely in the hopes that our teammates prove worthy of it. The second way we offer trust is by earning it over time. When my kids tell me to trust them (usually with a mischievous twinkle in their eyes), I recall our history and decide the likelihood that they are trustworthy in that moment.

Trust is also given in kinds. *Common trust* is what we give to one another as we live in a civil society together. I trust that you are going to stop at the red stop light. I trust that you will pay for the things you need instead of stealing them. I trust that when I bring my child to church they will be safe. I trust that when I make a donation to the church it will be used wisely. *Vulnerability-based trust* is the willingness to be completely open with one another and feel confident that your team members' intentions are good. As Brené Brown reminds us, "Vulnerability sounds like truth and feels like courage. Truth and courage aren't always comfortable, but they're never weakness."[3] The church, of all places, should be the space where we nurture vulnerability-based trust. We tell each other the truth of our lives: that our teenager is struggling with drug use, or we hate our job, or we are worried about our marriage. We ask for help when we are sick and need food or when we feel lost and alone and need friends to talk to. Vulnerability-based trust lets us admit our mistakes, ask for help, and feel that we are part of a team that has our backs no matter what. To me, that sounds a lot like how Paul talked about the body of Christ in 1 Corinthians 12:25–26:

> The way God designed our bodies is a model for understanding our lives together as a church: every part dependent on every other part, the parts we mention and the parts we don't, the parts we see and the parts we don't. If one part hurts, every other part is involved in the hurt, and in the healing. If one part flourishes, every other part enters into the exuberance. *(The Message)*

We are all in this together.

If you've ever been on a dysfunctional team (who hasn't, right?), you know that at the root of the dysfunction is a corrosive lack of trust between the members that generates misunderstood motivations, assumptions of ill-intent, disengagement, and sometimes sabotage. We start playing "Cards Against Humanity"-styled games with each other and end up causing enormous damage. In the hundreds of interviews I've done with church members while consulting, I have heard too many stories of really bad behavior: covering up mistakes, gossiping, hoarding information, leaking confidential information, micro-managing, sending mixed messages, shooting the messenger, shutting down others' ideas, taking credit for others' work, and throwing people under the bus. It's as heartbreaking as it is unacceptable.

One of my coaching clients, Susan, is the senior pastor of a large urban church on the East Coast. She previously served as the senior pastor for four other congregations before this one. When she took this job, she quickly discovered that she was working in a church with a long history of distrust at every level of leadership.

Most of her congregants were in their fifties and older and had been members of this church for over twenty years. They had run off three senior pastors before her. She was the first female senior pastor they had ever called. She had her work cut out for her.

Rebuilding trust in systems in which it has been absent for some time is a costly and long process. Where there is a lack of trust, there is also likely a fear of conflict, breeding passive-aggressive (and sometimes outright-aggressive) behavior. Where there is a fear of conflict, we often see a lack of commitment to the vision, to the mission, and, finally, to the faith community itself. Healthy people don't stick around in systems that reward unhealthy behavior. Once we start to see a lack of commitment in the strong leaders in the church, we quickly see the results: the community loses any sense of accountability to its vision or its people, and ceases to be a relevant, vital embodiment of the body of Christ in the world.

Susan knew that she had to start by rebuilding trust among her key leadership. She started by rebuilding the relational connections between them. For example, in the previous year, Hugh had told Sally that the children's program wasn't growing because she was in charge of it. She was devastated. Joan had lobbied the finance team to defund the homeless ministry that Tom directed just because they had a disagreement about whether or not homeless people could use the bathrooms in the church. With no money, Tom couldn't keep the ministry going. Don told everyone who would listen that he didn't like Susan's leadership as their senior pastor, because women weren't cut out to be pastors. Everywhere Susan turned, people were behaving in ways that caused enormous hurt between the leaders and members. Susan couldn't move forward until they began to address that. She was smart in how she proceeded, using a process that would benefit all. She worked with them through the following steps for reestablishing trust between people:

1. **Come clean about what you have done or neglected to do.** You made a mistake. Accept it. Trust will never be rebuilt if we aren't starting from a place of honesty and truth. Tell the truth, the whole truth, and nothing but the truth—with no excuses, explanations, or justifications. Own your actions.

2. **Be prepared for people to have feelings.** Feelings are not right or wrong, good or bad. It's what we do with them that matters. But be prepared for people to be emotionally triggered by your truth-telling. Whatever response they offer, it's the right one for them.

3. **Take responsibility for your actions.** You don't need to justify or explain yourself. Explanations are rarely helpful. You need to take responsibility for your actions, say what you will do differently in the future, and then do it.

4. **Make your actions as transparent as possible.** Because trust takes time to rebuild, people need time to see if your words match your actions. In the meantime, you may be met with suspicion or questions that feel invasive or distrustful of you. During this period, that's fair game. So, be as transparent as you can be. When people see you have nothing to hide, they stop looking.

5. **Don't get defensive.** Just because you are asking for forgiveness and stating your intention to do better doesn't mean you will be granted that forgiveness immediately and fully. Don't be defensive if people bring up past issues or name their fears. For this time, that is okay. At a point in the future, they will need to let it go. But you will both know when that time comes.

6. **Forgive yourself.** At the end of the day, you can't control other people's actions or reactions. You *can* control your own. Forgive yourself for causing harm. Recommit to making sure you don't do it again. Rinse and repeat.

My friend and fellow Center for Progressive Renewal board member, Glennon Doyle, founder of Together Rising, often says, "When we get close to each other, we stop being afraid. Fear can't survive proximity." Some of the most painful conversations I've mediated in churches are between well-meaning people who profoundly hurt one another because they made assumptions and feared the worst in a person. That fear creates a toxic reality that causes real harm. That's why knowing one another, trusting one another, and staying close is essential for a healthy congregation to thrive. We can't be a team otherwise.

How would you describe the health of your congregation today?

A Personal Practice

With the right support systems, we are all capable of accomplishing incredible feats. I want you to imagine your dream team for a project that you are working on. They don't have to be real people or living people; in fact, most of the time I prefer people I've never met but whose work I admire. What is it about them that makes you feel more creative? What do they teach you? Write down the people on your team.

Example: I'm working on writing this book. When I sat down to begin this project, I imagined the kind of team that I would need to draw on to get me through. Here are the people I recruited to my team (and they had no idea):

- Barack Obama – That man has a way with words! I am inspired by the way he can use words to cast a vision grand enough to power our nation and our world. His leadership has been a model for all of us.

- Martha Beck – Because I love her writing, and I've learned so much from her books. She seems like a fun person.

- Carl Jung – I am just exploring his work, but, "Wow!" It is blowing my mind. He's helping me get more honest with myself, to see myself more clearly, which is invaluable. I need him on the team.

- Mel Toomey – He's been my leadership coach for four years now, and everything he has taught me is woven throughout this book.

- Ruth Bader Ginsberg – Not only is she brilliant, but her work ethic drives her to sit at her desk (or the Bench) morning to night, Monday thru Friday, reading and writing briefs. Then she crashes and sleeps the entire weekend. Makes sense to me.

- Amelia Earhart – Because...*duh.*

- Bill Moyers – He was a brilliant journalist who took the time to look deeply at the world. I want to draw on his wisdom.

As I began my writing each day, I would welcome my team (in my head so that no one thought I was really crazy), and, then, as I was writing and got stuck, I would ask one of my team members to help me out. I imagined what they would say:

"You're not speaking from your heart, Cameron. Your writing is too distant, too intellectual. Why are you hiding?" Carl Jung would ask me.

"Look more closely, Cameron, and you will see the connections between theological structures and power structures that need to be called out," Bill Moyers would suggest.

"I know you don't feel like writing today, but this is your work. Get busy!" Ruth would push me on, adjusting one of her many "dissent collars" to sit correctly against her robe.

Each of these team members, and a few others that I would recruit for the day, became my accountability team and my inspirational support group. I could call on any or all of them when I needed help, and my imagination would come alive with the advice they would give.

You try it. You can recruit a dream team as I did, or you can approach real, living people you know personally. Rally your team around your project, and see what happens. I have the feeling it will blow you away.

A Congregational Practice

Here I will offer you two practices. The first is, using the exercise above, build out your congregational saints team. Who are the saints, living or dead, who, when invoked, inspire you to courageous action? Once you have them identified, build a small group curriculum series that you can do in groups or give to families to use at home encouraging congregants to explore why these people are inspiring and what they can learn from their example.

The second exercise is for those of you left-brained, analytical types. Let's explore the congregation's permission-giving culture when it comes to leadership and team membership. In a group, complete the following:

1   2

Y   N   It's normal practice for our church leadership teams to admit our mistakes and make amends if needed

N   Y   We have lost some of our best leaders because of disagreements or conflict

Y   N   We have no problem asking for help from each other

Y   N   We solve problems quickly and easily

Y   N   We feel comfortable taking risks by offering new ideas and/or giving helpful, sometimes challenging, feedback

N   Y   We fear failure so we tend to play it safe

Y   N   We can talk about difficult topics

Y   N   We support each other and work to bring out the best in one another

N   Y   We revisit discussions and past decisions over and over

Y   N   We appreciate process but we push against inefficiency and bureaucracy

N   Y   We aren't sure who we are or why we exist as a church…but we really like each other!

Y   N   We share a common mission and clear goals

Y   N   We celebrate our successes with one another and encourage each other along the way

If you circled more than three responses in column 2, then you have some work to do on building your health team.

Small Group Discussion Questions

1. Do you think your church attracts strong leaders and builds strong teams?

2. Do you personally feel that your contributions are recognized and valued?

3. Are people willing to be vulnerable and share what is working and not working in the church?

4. Do you as a congregation celebrate your achievements? Why or why not? How can you change?

5. How are you at having painful conversations?

---

[1] Quoted in Kimberly Weisul, "Jim Collins: Good to Great in 10 Steps," *Inc.*, https://www.inc.com/kimberly-weisul/jim-collins-good-to-great-in-ten-steps.html .

[2] Patrick Lencioni, *The Five Dysfunctions of a Team: A Leadership Fable* (San Francisco: Jossey Bass, 2002).

[3] Brené Brown, *Daring Greatly: How the Courage to Be Vulnerable Transforms the Way We Live, Love, Parent, and Lead* (New York: Avery, 2012), 37.

Chapter Five

Charting Your Course

"Flying is a great equalizer. The plane doesn't know or care about your gender as a pilot, nor do the ground troops who need your support. You just have to perform. That's all anyone cares about when you're up there—that you can do your job, and that you do it exceptionally well."
—Lt. Col. Christine Mau, 33rd Fighter Wing Operations Group Deputy Commander

Bessie Coleman knew the first time she saw a plane fly over the sharecropping field she and her family worked in Texas that she wanted to fly. She was a young African American girl born in 1892, before airplanes even existed. Staring up into the sky on that fateful day, she knew in her bones that if she was determined, focused, and lucky, she would be a pilot one day. It made no sense, of course. No black woman had ever dared to dream of such a thing. But she knew in the deepest part of herself that she was called to that life. She had just one major challenge: no flight schools in the United States would train an African American woman to fly.

In 1916, at the age of 24, Coleman moved to Chicago, Illinois, where she lived with her brothers. In Chicago, she worked as a manicurist at the White Sox Barber Shop. There she heard stories from pilots returning home from World War I. These stories only furthered fueled her passion. She could practically feel herself flying on their missions as they described the close calls, daring maneuvers, and exhilarating moments. She knew that opportunities for her to realize her dream in the United States were slim to none. Recognizing Coleman's talent and passion, Robert S. Abbott, founder and publisher of the *Chicago Defender,* encouraged her to study abroad. Coleman received financial backing from banker Jesse Binga and the *Defender* to study in France where she became the first African American woman to hold a pilot's license.

Hers is a remarkable story. After earning her license, Coleman returned to the United States and went on to become a stunt pilot, performing awe-inspiring maneuvers at airshows across the nation to earn a living. She became wildly popular and well-respected, named by other pilots as "the world's greatest woman flier." As a professional aviatrix, she gained a reputation as a skilled and daring pilot who would stop at nothing to complete a difficult stunt.

We wouldn't know about Bessie Coleman today if she had not charted her course early in life to become a pilot. She knew herself and believed in what she was capable of accomplishing. She was brave and tenacious. She committed herself to her calling and did what it took to achieve it. She paid a price and had to make a number of detours along the way. But today, she stands in our history books as the first female African American licensed pilot.

Where Are You Going?

It would be a shame if you allowed yourself to get away with merely existing, coasting along through life with no focus or vision for making a positive difference. Even if you later decide to change course, take some time now to decide where you think you want to go. What is your destination? What story do you want to tell about your life journey? You can get through life without a flight plan, but what a waste! You are capable of so much more.

When I ask my coaching clients what they would like to be able to say about themselves one year from now, most of them struggle to respond. They give me institutional answers:

"I want to be the senior pastor of a church with 500 members."

"I want to be the person the media calls about faith issues in our community."

"I want our congregation grow by 25 percent, with families with young children."

"I want to be the president/senior warden/board chair of our congregation."

"I want to have more control of my time and not feel like I am running from meeting to meeting."

These responses tell me what they want to be *doing* one year from now. They don't tell me anything about who they want to be, how they want to grow, what they want to manifest in themselves. They are trained to define their value by their "doing." They can tap into genuine power when they also invest in their "being." Predictably, I get responses that these leaders think they should say to me. What I want them to tap into is the energy behind the response, the feelings that come up when they imagine who they are and where they are one year from now. When they can *feel* their future, visualizing it not just with their head but feeling it in their body, sensing the "rightness" (or "wrongness") of it and the resonance in their soul, then we know that we are onto something meaningful. They have tapped into the power available to all of us to manifest our present and future in ways deeply aligned with who we are. That is when transformational personal and congregational growth can occur.

How NOT to Start

Most "course-charting exercises" in the mainline church begin with laborious research and surveys and studies. We process the hell out of our systems, producing lovely reports with lots of colorful graphs. Sometimes these are helpful. I'm not knocking them, having produced quite a few myself. But it is the wrong place to start. We see what we are looking for in data and research. We need to be sure we have done the work to have the "eyes to see and the ears to hear" new insights, possibilities, and patterns.

Bessie Coleman set her course in a moment of inspiration, when she felt her soul commit to flying. She started with an inner knowing. We can learn from that. Instead of starting with research and reports, start from a place of meditation or prayer. Believe me, I'm not all that pious; however, significant scientific research has proven that meditation and prayer shift your consciousness from a state of rapid pattern association and "flight or flight" energy to one of rest, relaxation, and playfulness. When your mind shifts its energy to a space of calm creativity, you experience an opening in yourself that becomes essential to all breakthrough thinking.

Dr. Jill Bolte Taylor, a neuroanatomist at Harvard Medical School, wrote about this in her book *My Stroke of Insight*. At the age of thirty-seven, she experienced a stroke that wiped out the speech center in the left side of her brain. Because of her medical training, she was able to observe what was happening to her, though it took her many years after that to be able to write about it. When you lose the ability to think in language (when the left hemisphere of your brain goes "offline"), you rely entirely on the capacities of the right hemisphere. Our right hemisphere, as Dr. Taylor teaches us in her TED talk—which you should watch (google "Jill Bolte Taylor TED talk")—is all about the present moment. It processes in pictures and learns kinesthetically through the movement of our bodies. It experiences the present moment all at once—what it feels like, smells like, looks like, tastes like, sounds like—and processes it through this explosive energetic collage that it calls "now," or the "present moment." We become aware of our connection to each other and our world through our right hemispheres.

She later describes her purely right hemisphere experience by saying, "I felt enormous and expansive. I felt at one with all of the energy that was, and it was beautiful." Without the bounds of language, she came to the realization that we all have access to a part of ourselves that understands our interconnectedness to all things. When we finally realize that, she said, we also realize that, "We are perfect. We are whole. And we are beautiful."

That is what prayer does for us. Prayer helps us tap into the part of ourselves that understands energy, that trusts our connection to each other and our planet. Prayer helps us see new energetic patterns and new possibilities. Prayer is not some weird magical trick to manipulate God into giving us what we want. Prayer is the practice of opening ourselves to the world beyond language that reminds us that we are all One.

Here is why this matters: deep change or growth in our congregations comes faster, easier, and more joyfully when we start from a space of open imagination. Prayer is the practice we use in our tradition to access that space.

When you start the work of charting your course in your life or in your congregation, I strongly suggest that you start with opening yourself and listening. My friend and colleague Martha Grace Reese[1] wrote four books about congregational renewal in which she suggested that the single most important practice in a congregation's life together was praying together. Whatever process that followed would be grounded and have power because it started from practicing this deep wordlessness.

As you start the discernment journey, I suggest that you make space for times of prayer and reflection throughout your process. In some congregations I work with, I start with 90 days of prayer and reflection, during which people gather in small groups to build and strengthen friendships. Committee work is forbidden. I ask people to make prayer or meditation a regular part of their day. I ask them to teach this to their children, and make it a part of their family life. Again, this isn't because I think it has some magical power. I *know* it helps us focus our energy, open our minds, and recognize our connections. When we are in that space, anything becomes possible.

Opening Your Focus

Let's try an exercise that Princeton researcher Les Fehmi designed and explains in his book *The Open Focus Brain*.[2]

1. Stand, sit, or lie down, and focus your eyes on an object in front of you.

2. Without moving your head or eyes, broaden your attention until you register everything in your field of vision, including the original object that you were focused on.

3. Still without moving your head or eyes, make the object the foreground of your attention and everything else the background.

4. Next, make the object the background and everything else the foreground.

5. Focus on everything in your vision field at once while repeating to yourself, "Everything, all of it, we are one."

By doing this exercise, you are opening your perspective. You are reminding yourself that everything is already in relationship. Your job is simply to see the patterns and sense the connections. Being conscious of our interdependence gives you the depth of grounding you need to lead forward with the wisdom of an elder. You see a longer game and draw on deeper insights already within you. When you operate from a busy or distracted space, you can't access the deeper wisdom within yourself. You are lucky if you can remember your name! But when you slow down, breathe, broaden your perspective, and reconnect with the ongoing, unfolding Story, you sense your next steps. It's as if they rise up to meet you. Try it. I promise it works.

Flight Planning

You start every flight by reviewing your maps. If you are flying VFR (Visual Flight Rules), you carefully study the VFR map, looking at obstacles or complicated airspace that you might encounter on your route. When flying VFR, you are not required to file a flight plan or notify anyone of where you are going. You can just jump in a plane and go. While that has its appeal, it also demands a higher level of preparation to be safe. The other option is to fly IFR (Instrument Flight Rules), which you can only do if you are an instrument-rated pilot. Flying IFR means that you let air traffic control know your departure and arrival airports, an estimated time of departure, the number of people on board, the type of airplane you are flying, and the altitude you request. It's a lot more detailed than just jumping in the plane! If you fly IFR, you need Air Traffic Control clearance before you take off so that they can track your flight the entire way, ensuring that you stay on course and clear of traffic along the route.

To chart a course in previous eras, pilots would pull out large paper maps and draw their routes using a pencil and ruler. Today, we open our iPads. In the program I use, I have access to suggestions from other pilots about the best way to fly to my destination. They have already done the work to divert the flight around restricted airspace and sometimes even suggest a preferred altitude based on obstacles and terrain. I can use their flight plan or make my own. Either way, reviewing their flight plans informs my planning.

When I get to the airport, I make sure to talk with other pilots who have flown just before me. I want to know if I should expect any weather or turbulence that might not show up in my weather briefings. I also ask them about any airport information that I might have missed. It's amazing what you discover by talking to people.

That's how I would suggest you start after you have opened your focus and taken time for mediation and prayer. You need to start engaging people. In this next phase of your "course charting," let's imagine that we are flying one long trip by planning four connecting legs. We will use the acronym RIDE to describe each leg of the flight:

R Review current and historical documents

I Interview congregation members and community leaders

D (Study the) Demographics for your area using open source data and available proprietary reports

E Evaluate what you have learned and identify the themes

Doing this research ensures that you understand your context—your terrain—as you are planning your journey. Let's explore each one:

Leg 1: Review Current and Historical Documents

Just as many of us keep journals that document the ebbs and flows of our personal lives, congregations also have documents that tell a story about their journey over time. These documents are invaluable to getting to the heart of the congregational culture. As you start digging, look for these specific storylines:

1. **Budgets, Investments, and Risk:** What have been the financial trends of the congregation over time? Does the congregation tend to make long-term or short-term investments? Does it pay everything off or is it comfortable carrying loans? How much money has the

congregation raised through capital campaigns? Does your church track cash flow? How are budgets built and who decides? What percentage of the budget is supported by large donations from single donors?

2. **Newsletters, websites, and other communication pieces:** What themes do you see in the communication pieces as you look at them over time? What messages do you get from the stories highlighted and ministries promoted? Who is left out? Do you see any shifts in priorities over time? Do you sense the congregation communicating messages it shouldn't? Is the story it's telling on the website true to who the congregation is and wants to be?

3. **Membership and attendance trends:** Churches define membership and attendance in various ways. Sometimes they just track the number of members who stand up on a Sunday and officially join. Other times, churches might track anyone who attends regardless of membership. It actually doesn't matter what you track, but for research purposes, do your best to make sure you are looking at a consistent metric. Next, chart the membership and attendance numbers on a line graph. What do you notice about the change over the years? What stories emerge that might involve periods of growth or conflict/decline? Is there a "growth ceiling" that the church hits over and over (*example:* the church gets to about 200 active participants and then has a crisis...over and over)? Does it fire its pastor at predictable intervals? If you want to be ambitious, partner with a similar local congregation in your community and compare your data to theirs. Are there communitywide patterns that impact you both?

Leg 2: Interview Congregation Members and Community Leaders

Now, get ready to have some fun! I recommend that you gather interviews in three ways: in-person interviews with key leaders and stakeholders in the congregation, in-person or phone interviews of community leaders, and an online congregational assessment. You might consider recruiting a team of interviewers for this phase so that you can gather more data and stories. You also need to consider that, in some interviews, people might share sensitive information that should remain confidential. If you do recruit a team, make sure they understand the ground rules and have the credibility to carry them out.

1. **Congregational Interviews:** I usually set up 30-minute interviews with congregation members and complete them over a three-day

period. If you have just one person doing the interviews, you will be able to complete about 35 interviews. The number you want to complete depends entirely on the size of the congregation. Usually 1–2 interviewers completing between 30 and 50 interviews is sufficient. You will want to ask some standard questions, with follow up questions that only become clear as the interview progresses. Here are suggested questions:

a. What brought you to this church and why do you stay?

b. What hopes do you have for our future?

c. What concerns do you have that may be in our way?

d. What should I have asked you had I known you better?

Either record these conversations (with permission) or take as close to exact dictation as possible in these conversations. Write down direct quotes from them when you hear something interesting or helpful. Listen for themes and be sure to write them down. After you have completed the interviews, you will see clear themes (waypoints) that become the basis for your strategy design later.

2. **Community Leader Interviews:** Interviewing business, government, NGO, and other community leaders gives you invaluable insight about your congregation and its possible contribution to the community in the future. Make a list of the community leaders you believe might have some insight into your congregation and its role in the community. Make sure you have a diverse list. You will want people such as the local school administrator/principal, real estate agents, local business owners, city officials from government and law enforcement, leaders of community nonprofits, parents from the local parenting group, etc. Set up interviews with them and use the following template:

   a. **Tell me how you came to do what you do in this community.** You are getting to know one another and sharing your stories. Listen for the experiences that shape his/her/their perspective. To the extent that it is possible and authentic, share some of your own personal story to establish a baseline of relationship and trust at the beginning of the interview.

   b. **How have you observed this community changing over the past few years?** Listen for the changes that they name; those usually point to fear points or personal priorities. Also, listen for how they describe the change. Are they hopeful and encouraged by what they are seeing? Are they sad and fearful?

c. **How might we make our community stronger?** Listen for what "stronger" means to them. Again, it reveals what matters to them. Also listen for their level of investment in being part of the team. If they are using "you/them/they" language, they may not be personally invested. If they are using "I/we/us" language, they might be future partners.

d. **I am asking you these questions because I am a member of a church that wants to make a positive difference in this community. What do you wish we would do/invest in/ create? What advice would you give us?**

While I suggest following this template, every community is different. If these questions don't seem right, ask other ones. You are trying to discern the wisdom and insight these leaders have for your church. As long as you are eliciting that from the conversation, keep going!

3. **Online Congregational Assessment:** Most online congregational assessment tools measure the internal dynamics of church members—attendance patterns; personal spiritual practices; opinions about leadership, programming, and direction. Almost all of them fail to measure the difference the church is making in the wider community. I've often said that if a church is to have a viable future, it must be committed to raising the standard of life for the people living in its surrounding community. If we are going to obsess about attendance at a Sunday service and giving patterns, then we should also obsess about graduation rates, employment rates, debt loads, drug use, and oppressive legislation, to name a few areas. In an effort to study all such factors, the Center for Progressive Renewal, of which I am a founder, with the assistance of Rev. Dr. Anna Hall, designed an assessment that gets at this information in a balanced way that shows the relationship between internal health and external impact. To find out more, go to http://www. progressiverenewal.org. I would encourage you to use this tool or one similar to it to ensure that you are getting the widest input possible from your larger congregation.

Leg 3: Study the Demographics

You can collect demographic information in many ways. Doing a search for your area code in the U.S. Census online system (https://factfinder. census.gov) or City Data (http://www.city-data.com) will give you a good start in seeing the demographic trends in your area. You might also work with a company such as Mission Insite (http://www.missioninsite.com)

to run specific reports for your area. Often, denominational offices will have contracts with demographic companies and can run these reports for you for free. These reports are designed to give you insights into the general trends of people in your area: age, race, income and education level, housing, and political affiliation. These numbers can also tell you about who your future members might be.

I was working with a theologically progressive church in Miami, and we discovered that there were 453,584 people living in their area of Miami-Dade, Florida, at that time. We also learned that 287,572 of them voted for democratic candidates in the last election. I realize that we can't say that people who are theologically progressive always vote for a democrat, but it's likely a high percentage. These people became our target population to study.

The challenge was that we couldn't fit all 287,572 people into the building if we got them all to church, so we needed a smaller number to engage. We decided that we would try to connect with just 10 percent of those people, which turns out to be 28,757. The church really only holds about 350 people comfortably, so we had to go even smaller. We decided that we wanted to study just 1 percent of the 10 percent, which was 287 people.

Finally, a number we could manage! Do notice that we basically wrote off 99.9 percent of the people who voted for a democrat living in that area and decided to deep-dive into connecting with .1 percent of the progressive neighbors through outreach efforts. When you use data this way, suddenly growing a congregation becomes a fun numbers game.

Leg 4: Put It All Together

At this point, you may feel like you have so much data that you now need to deploy IBM's WATSON Big Data analytic computer to draw any meaning from it all. Not to worry. Let's put it all together. Most mainline church people like to distill their information into fancy reports, so I will walk you through that process. If you are in a congregation that would rather dance, write poetry, develop videos, or design crossword puzzles as a way to distill this information to the larger congregation, go for it! The delivery method doesn't matter; the message just needs to get out.

Structure your document in these key sections:

- The Process
- Church Data
- Community Demographics
- Interview Themes
- Areas of Recommended Focus

In "The Process" section, tell the story of why you are doing this work at all. What happened to make you want to "chart a flight" in the first place? Who was involved in the work? How and why did you decide on the process you did? You want to give some background to people reading the report so that they have context for all that follows.

In the "Church Data" section, highlight the significant trends you discovered about the congregants. Include the church attendance and giving graphs that you developed earlier. Talk about the general demographic information of the current membership—percentage in various age ranges, races, gender identities, sexual orientations, income levels, education levels, etc. List any significant ministries of the church and the difference they make in the community. Include quotes from your interviews but *do not* attribute them to specific people. Say something such as: "One member described the congregation's recent conflict as 'a healthy process in which we disagreed and still found a way to move forward. I was really proud of our church.'" Written this way, no one can identify or attribute the quote to a specific person, but the power of the statement still serves as an illustration of a critical point of insight.

In the "Community Demographics" section, highlight the significant trends that are and will impact the church going forward—number of people moving into or out of the community, general income levels, housing options, education options, etc. Compare them to what you know about your congregation. Are there interesting gaps between who comes to church and those living in the community? Here, you might also include quotes from the community leaders that you interviewed to underscore the themes you see emerging. You may discover some statistics that point to a turbulent future ahead—people moving away from your area or major businesses closing. While this might not be the news you want to read, you need to factor it into your planning.

In the "Interview Themes" section, distill the interviews into 3–5 dominant theme categories. Based on the hundreds of interviews I have completed, I've started to see common themes that include communication, visitor retention, financial sustainability, conflict, leadership and management, vision, and mission. A "theme" only exists if you hear it in three or more interviews. You must be cautious to not allow outlier agendas to influence your reporting. Write down what people are saying based on these themes, being careful to protect identities and only focus on themes that help the church move forward.

In the "Areas of Recommended Focus," you bring it all together. What are the themes running through all of the sections that need to be highlighted? If the neighborhood is growing, but the church is declining and many of the people said they couldn't figure out why people visit but don't come back, you likely need to focus on visitor retention. If the building was built in 1922, the church is sustaining it's professional staff by spending down the endowment, and your interviews reveal that members are worried that families with young children aren't coming to the church, you likely are looking at an issue of financial sustainability.

It's like a puzzle, putting the pieces of what you learned together to find a pattern of meaning that is actionable for your future. Don't manipulate the data; listen to it and learn what it can teach you. A word of advice from my experience: write this report as an inspirational guide for the future. No one is edified by negative or critical language. Ultimately, you are doing this work because you want to ensure your congregation's best days are ahead. Use this exercise as a way to help members dream, and then take the next best steps toward a meaning-filled future.

A Personal Practice: Taking a Life Assessment

You might have guessed that the process I've outlined above could also apply to your personal life—with some tweaks.

1. Start by grounding yourself with meditation or prayer. Find your core and anchor yourself. This becomes especially important because, if you are one to be influenced or driven by the opinions of others, doing a life assessment can be disorienting and possibly harmful. You want to be sure you are secure enough in your own being to know what feedback to accept and what to throw away.

2. If you are someone who writes in a journal regularly, take some time to look back over the years at your reflections. What themes do you see? What is happening in your life when you feel powerful? What about when you feel weak? Are there types of people you have in your life even if the specific individuals come and go (a father figure, a guru, a bully, a dependent)? If you don't write in a journal, perhaps you have a file with letters, cards, awards, and other meaningful pieces of paper that tell a story about you. Or, look back through your digital photos over the last many years. Where are you? What are you doing? Who are you with? What do you see as trends driving your life?

3. Next, talk to people who might have some wisdom for you. Ask your friends, colleagues, and family about what they hope for your future. What makes them proud of you? What inspires them about you? What makes them worry? A word of caution here: Not every opinion is valid. If you don't have a good relationship with someone, don't engage them with this exercise. If you have a friend who is "life-taking" and makes everything about themselves, don't ask them to contribute to this practice. Be wise about who you approach and hold what they offer you both reverently and loosely. They are not making predictions about your life; they are

offering observations. You get to decide what kind of influence they ultimately have in your life.

4. Think of people who inspire you—famous people or people that you know in your life. What do they do that you find inspiring? What have they had to overcome? What drives them? How and who do they influence? What values do they embody? Now, think about yourself. Do you see yourself in them?

Next, write down or record what you have learned. You might write it as a letter to yourself that you can read over the coming years. You might create a video in which you talk out your learnings. You might write a poem or paint a picture or choreograph a dance. You might write a short story. Do what feels the most freeing and the more natural to you. This becomes a gift you give yourself, an anchoring moment that you can come back to later as you set out on new adventures. Come back to it often and remember what you have learned about who you are in this moment, to use as an inspiration for who you are becoming.

A Congregational Practice: 90 Days of Small Group Discernment

Jesus modeled how we are changed and how we change the world by gathering a small group, being open and vulnerable with them, and connecting them in a new community. I invite you as a congregation to take up the challenge of spending 90 days in discernment in small groups. You will meet once every two weeks and, after starting your time with centering prayer or quiet meditation, focus each session on one of the following questions:

1. Who is God? Who are we?

2. Who are our neighbors?

3. What are the gifts, passions, and deepest longings of our members and our neighbors?

4. What are we willing to offer to make possible God's calling in our church?

5. What are we willing to do to bring to life God's calling in our church?

6. What are we willing to let go of to make room for God's calling in our church?

At the end of the 90 days, review what you learned about yourselves. You might host a congregational event after worship one Sunday or designate a special event/retreat over a weekend. Inevitably, the insights that come through these conversations will influence the direction your congregation takes going forward.

Small Group Discussion Questions

1. What is the highest and best use of our time, talent, and funds as a congregation at this point?

2. What am I afraid to learn about our church in a process such as this?

3. What makes us different from a secular nonprofit?

4. What difference could we make in our community that would raise the quality of life for everyone?

---

[1] Martha Grace Reese wrote four books often referred to as the "Unbinding Series," in which she explores the dynamics of congregational renewal and personal spiritual growth. You can find out more about them by going to chalicepress.com.

[2] Les Fehmi, *The Open-Focus Brain: Harnessing the Power of Attention to Heal Mind and Body* (Boston: Trumpeter, 2007).

Chapter Six

Preflight Checklist

Checklist

- ❑ Verify your weight and balance calculations, and known runway lengths
- ❑ Inspect the plane thoroughly inside and out
- ❑ Get the latest weather forecast
- ❑ Brief the passengers on the safety regulations

"Bravery comes along as a gradual accumulation of discipline."
—Buzz Aldrin, US Astronaut on the Apollo 11 mission

I always arrive at the airfield at least one hour before I am scheduled to take off. This gives me time to complete my pre-flight checklist, file my flight plans to let air traffic control know when I'm leaving and where I'm heading, double-check the weather to make sure I don't hit potentially devastating storms during the flight, and, of course, inspect my plane.

I walk out to the ramp where my plane sits among a fleet of others tied down in a row. I walk around the nose of the plane and pat the propeller, as if saying, "Hi 823MC, we are going to be in this together today." It's my passive-aggressive way of asking the plane to be on its best behavior.

The plane inspection involves many steps that some pilots might be tempted to short-change or skip. After all, pilots do the same inspection regimen over and over with each flight. However, experienced pilots will tell you that skipping over any part of this checklist is a reckless mistake. There is no room for laziness in piloting a plane.

The pre-flight checklist involves three phases:

- Visual inspection of the plane;

- Mechanical inspection of the instrument panel, radio, radar, flaps, rudder, stabilizer, fuel pressure, and engine;

- Flight plan review—double-checking fuel consumption calculations, weight distribution, etc.

Skipping any of these steps jeopardizes your safety and the safety of the people on the ground should things not go well. You don't want to be "that guy" who forgot to check the fuel and made national news by landing on the freeway. Honestly, that is my worst nightmare. If you ever see me on the news, you will know that was the most embarrassing day of my life.

The Four Systems for Flight

In the last chapter, we "planned our flight" by using research tools and processing what we learned into areas of recommendations for our congregation. That research told us where we are now, where we could go, and what could hold us back. With our destination in mind, we need to ensure that our plane can get us there. We can plan the perfect flight on paper, but if our plane breaks or our crew quits, we won't make it to our destination.

I was working with a large, established downtown church in Washington, D.C. They wanted to design a plan for the next five years of their congregational life and sent me copies of previous plans they had developed as models for our work together. Here is what I read:

Our Mission:
Empowered by the Spirit and guided by Holy Scripture, we are called to be a community of worship, welcome, spiritual formation, and reconciliation.

Our Goals:
1. *Integrate intentional theological reflection into all service opportunities*

2. *Strengthen our worship tradition by welcoming and affirming a wider diversity of people*

3. *Expand technological means through which worship services may be shared with others*

4. *Initiate pulpit and choir exchanges with diverse congregations*

5. *Celebrate the Lord's Supper more frequently in worship*

6. *Provide theological and practical training for ushers, greeters, and members on becoming even more of an invitational community*

7. *Participate actively in neighborhood associations*

8. *Encourage attendance and leadership at denominational conferences and gatherings*

9. *Develop a comprehensive educational plan for children and youth with specific learning goals for each year*

10. *Expand our understanding and practice of Christian hospitality*

All of these are fine goals, but they are not strategic. It's not at all clear that they outline actions that move the congregation closer to its mission in measurable ways. Many churches fall into this trap of confusing strategy with goal setting. The goals and action steps listed here are at best loosely connected to the mission statement above.

Your congregation needs four distinct systems working in strategic alignment together: theology, purpose, programs, and operations.

Theology: What stories does the congregation tell about its relationship to God and God's relationship to it?

Purpose: How does the congregation want to change the community?

Programs: What ministries exist to ensure that change in the world?

Performance: What systems, policies, and personnel are needed?

These represent parts of a whole that can provide a framework for designing congregational strategy. We often toss around phrases such as "strategic planning" and "organizational development," but then list some short-term goals that only address one of these four areas and have little to offer in unifying the whole. Instead, let's recognize that each of these systems benefits from its own strategies, which must be imagined within the environment in which they function and be in relationship to the rest.

Theology

The stories we tell ourselves about God, the world, and each other are bound in theological wrappings. These stories—Adam and Eve in the garden of Eden, the apocalypse and end times, Jesus' resurrection, Jonah and the whale, David and Bathsheba—shape our cultural imagination about what is important, who has power, who matters, how to behave, what to value. If you believe that the story of Adam and Eve gives us permission to dominate and subdue the earth, the chances are good you have little value for environmental protection. If you believe that God is an old white man with a long beard who passes his power through men, you likely don't support women's rights issues or women in leadership in your church. If you believe that the Bible condemns homosexuality as the final word on human sexual expression, you likely don't want gay and lesbian folks coming to your church. Your theology drives the shape of your congregation.

In our current political climate, congregations need to be clear about their theology. Are poor people cursed by God? Do you advocate for LGBTQ people? Do you believe the Bible is the inerrant word of God? Do you think we should protect the earth or dominate and consume it? How should we talk about resurrection? Should men be the heads of households? How do we talk about miracles, demons, angels, God, the Holy Spirit? What did Jesus mean when he said, "I am the way, and the truth, and the life..." (Jn. 14:6a)? While these seem like random and irrelevant questions, they form the basis of our social contract and how we treat one another.

Rev. Shawna Bowman, the pastor of Friendship Presbyterian Church in Chicago, Illinois, is one of the most gifted pastors with whom I have the privilege of working. With tattooed arms and hair that seems to be a different color every month, she has an artist's heart and a poet's mind. I've decided this is what makes her so brave—she sees the brokenness of the world, but she refuses to look away until she sees and captures its beauty for us in her art. Her congregation meets each Sunday in a quaint train station in a suburb of Chicago, where she leads them in worship by weaving together ancient liturgy and modern prayers. Recently, she had members of the congregation write a Lord's Prayer that felt authentic and real to them:

The New Lord's Prayer

(Rendered by and for Friendship Presbyterian Church)

Our Mothering, Guiding Moral Force, Gracious and Loving, Creator,

Who is our strength and shield and promises never to leave or forsake us,

who enfolds us and is all around us, in heaven and earth.

Blessed and cherished, divine and wondrous, and powerful are you.

May your purpose and everlasting presence,

your dream and vision of a world of peace, come to be.

And may your hope for us be realized on earth as it is in heaven.

Give each one of us enough to sustain all of us.

In our imperfections, we ask for forgiveness

for ourselves and from one another.

Save us from ourselves, from the bondage of selfishness,

from the distraction of prideful pursuits.

Help us to find the best of our human selves and to love that which others reject.

For all that you have created, the beauty and grace and the glory is yours forever.

Amen. (So be it.)

Churches all across the nation are waking up to the power of creating liturgies that speak to our present world. The practice becomes the theological clay that shapes our lives. For a lot of us, the practice become one of letting go of beliefs about God and the Bible that have not served us well, beliefs that give power to patriarchy, racism, classism, ableism, anti-Semitism, ageism, and heterosexism. These biases are rooted in us at early ages and too often justified by theological frames. When we see their flaws and let go of them, the openness left in their place becomes the fertile ground upon which we might sow a new, better, more mature understanding of who God is and who we are in relationship. This process is critical to awakening a consciousness is all of us, reminding us that we are loved by God and called to love one another.

Purpose

Hopefully your congregation—and you individually—wants to make a difference in the world in particular ways. Being clear about that helps you stay focused on keeping the "main thing the main thing." Creating a purpose framework, a set of rhetorical tools that hold your "big message" about who you are and what you do, focuses your actions going forward.

Many organizations create vision statements as a starting place. *Vision statements* describe the clear and inspirational long-term change you want to make as a result of your work. It could be that you want to end homelessness. Maybe you want to save the elephants. Maybe you are the person who will hold the world record for skydiving in a clown costume. The difference you want to make is up to you. You just need to be clear about what you are committed to and where you are going. Here are some vision statements that drive organizations you might recognize:

- **Human Rights Campaign**: Equality for everyone

- **Feeding America**: A hunger-free America

- **Oxfam**: A just world without poverty (five words)

- **The Nature Conservancy**: To leave a sustainable world for future generations

- **Make-A-Wish**: That people everywhere will share the power of a wish

- **Habitat for Humanity**: A world where everyone has a decent place to live

- **NPR,** with its network of independent member stations, is America's pre-eminent news institution

A *mission statement,* on the other hand, describes what you do. It describes how your actions will impact the world. Consider:

- **Human Rights Campaign:** Working to achieve lesbian, gay, bisexual, and transgender equality

- **Feeding America**: To feed America's hungry through a nationwide network of member food banks and engage our country in the fight to end hunger

- **Oxfam**: To create lasting solutions to poverty, hunger, and social injustice

- **The Nature Conservancy**: To conserve the lands and waters on which all life depends

- **Make-A-Wish:** We grant the wishes of children with life-threatening medical conditions to enrich the human experience with hope, strength, and joy

- **Habitat for Humanity:** Seeking to put God's love into action, Habitat for Humanity brings people together to build homes, communities, and hope

- **NPR**: To work in partnership with member stations to create a more informed public—one challenged and invigorated by a deeper understanding and appreciation of events, ideas, and cultures

These statements only matter if you put them at the heart of all you do. A *USA Today* article noted that the advertising slogan "Like a Rock" became the slogan that transformed the Chevy truck brand from being seen as unreliable to being top sellers in the nation.[1] The employees of the company had the image of a rock in their heads as they designed and produced the trucks. This created a new self-image for the company that was credited with its turnaround.

Let's try a vision-framing exercise. My colleague, Brian McLaren, posed a question to a group of us recently:

If we ask, "Which possible future is most morally, ethically, and spiritually desirable, and how can we contribute?" would we experience a better future than if we ask, "Which possible future is most likely, and how can we prepare and adjust?"

I appreciated his nuance. One gives us power; the other brings anxious paralysis. Keeping in mind Albert Einstein's observation, "Imagination is everything," play with the following:

1. Describe the kinds of relationships you wish your church had with:

    a. Church members

    b. Children

    c. Teenagers

    d. First-time visitors

    e. Local business leaders

    f. Government leaders

    g. Other churches

    h. Teachers

    i. Healthcare workers

(Complete the following statements…)

2. You wish your church invested more in…

3. You wish your church divested of…

4. You want your church to strengthen your community by…

Write down your responses. Reviewing your notes, write a first attempt at a vision statement that holds what you want to feel and accomplish as a congregation.

Programs

All congregations have a set of activities/ministries that become the delivery systems for the vision framework. Most congregations, however, are not particularly disciplined about making sure that they are aligned with the larger story of the difference the church wants to make in the world. Instead, they hold the annual yard sale because Mary Sue, who started it twelve years ago, still enjoys hosting it today. Larry still runs the adult Sunday school program because he was named the coordinator in 1979 and likes the program he put in place then. Change is hard.

If you have gone through the exercises of asking the big questions raised by your theological commitments and your vision framework, you should take the next best step: program alignment. It's in this phase that your vision statement shapes your mission statement and priorities. Here are some questions you might ask:

1. What programs or experiences could we offer to most effectively manifest our vision?

2. What are we uniquely qualified to provide?

3. What would be the easiest to deliver within the bounds of our current financial and human capacity?

4. What programs would provide longer-term sustainability?

Rev. Tom Bennet was the new senior pastor of a Presbyterian church. He knew that the church (which had hired him six months earlier) was burning out its best leaders with too many activities. He also knew that many of the ministries in the church didn't make sense if you looked at what the church said that it wanted to be in its vision statement. Together, we led the congregation though the vision framework process. They wrote the following mission statement: "We are a church committed to welcoming the rejected, fighting for the voiceless, and supporting the faithful in the name of Jesus Christ." We then asked: "Based on this statement and the difference we want to make in our community, what programs do we need to invest in? What can we let go?"

We gathered for a full day retreat in a beautiful room that overlooked a lake, the most inspiring scene you could imagine. That became a helpful counterbalance as I realized that the congregational leaders filling the room were completely stressed. No program leaders wanted to "give up" their program or dismantle their committee. But they had made a stand about who they said they were in their mission statement. They couldn't be everything to everyone.

To walk them through this, I put all of the ministries on different Post-It Notes and stuck them to the wall in front of us. Then I started grouping them under the phrases defined in their mission statement. I put their outreach ministry to autistic families under the "Welcome the Rejected" phrase. I added their education ministries to the "Supporting the Faithful" phrase. One by one, we went through the list until we had sorted the ones that made sense and then had a side pile of ones that didn't. The process made it clear to those leading the ministries not in the categories that they were not in alignment with the future direction of the church.

We then took a step back to ask Brian McLaren's question: *Which possible future is most morally, ethically, and spiritually desirable* (based on our mission), *and how can we contribute?* This gave us space to imagine new ministries or think of ways to improve the ones they had. The creativity was palpable. By the time we left the retreat center, we had designed an aligned programmatic strategy that was realistic and would make a difference.

Performance

Organizational fitness makes or breaks our success in the end. We might have the best vision in the world and the most talented people in the congregation, but if our database is a mess, or we can't accept online donations, or we have no accountability with our staff teams, we won't be able to bring our vision to life.

Churches in general are behind the curve on basic performance indicators. So many congregations that I work with are still tracking their membership and visitors on spreadsheets instead of CRM (client relationship management) database systems. Their websites were updated two years ago. They track their finances with inconsistent charts of accounts. They don't have job descriptions for the staff and did the last job review in 1998! As you assess your organizational performance, start with these questions:

1. What systems, policies, and procedures do we need in place to be well-run and in compliance with laws?

2. What are our human, financial, and facilities resource requirements for the coming years?

3. What are our long-term cash, capital, and staffing needs?

4. What operational information do our leaders need to make good decisions?

These "big picture" questions give you a scope of focus for performance readiness. You might consider drawing an organizational staffing chart with position titles, free from naming specific people. Run future financial scenarios accounting for major building renovations and/or staff expansion. These imaginative exercises serve two purposes: They expand your imagination about what is possible for your future, and they expose areas of vulnerability.

Strategy Spinout Checklist

In the early years of starting the Center for Progressive Renewal, we had the luxury of saying "yes" to a lot of experiments. We had a huge vision framework committed to renewing the mainline church, and lots of agility in our structure to test new ideas. We used to talk about "throwing things against the wall to see what sticks," and "building the plane while flying it." These were fun years, until they weren't.

At a staff meeting one afternoon, feeling the exhaustion of constant travel, writing, speaking, and meeting, we made a list of all of the programs we had developed and tested in the previous four years. We made a list of all of the partners we had recruited, the presentations we had given, the online courses we had designed, and the resources we had developed. The numbers were staggering...and unsustainable for our small team.

A member of our team who had been a former CEO of a Fortune 500 company had been at that point before. He recognized the spin that we were in. He said, "We need a spinout checklist." Quickly, he sketched out a model for us to use. We have adapted it over years of use, and now use it with congregations and individual coaching clients.

When you are considering new programs, partnerships, or priorities, use this spinout checklist to ensure that you are being strategic rather than just "busy."

Strategy Spinout Checklist Our Vision: Our Mission:			
	Opportunity A	Opportunity B	Opportunity C
Does it align with our vision and mission?	☐ Yes ☐ No	☐ Yes ☐ No	☐ Yes ☐ No
Does it require reasonable and acceptable levels of resources?	☐ Yes ☐ No	☐ Yes ☐ No	☐ Yes ☐ No
Will it yield results that are measurable and sustainable?	☐ Yes ☐ No	☐ Yes ☐ No	☐ Yes ☐ No
Will it financially break even or produce a surplus within 12 months (or have a source of dedicated funding)?	☐ Yes ☐ No	☐ Yes ☐ No	☐ Yes ☐ No
Will it put us in competition with other nonprofits or undermine our commitment to partnership?	☐ Yes ☐ No	☐ Yes ☐ No	☐ Yes ☐ No

Will it reinforce the community's view of us as a vital, mission-oriented church?	☐ Yes ☐ No	☐ Yes ☐ No	☐ Yes ☐ No

This checklist may have literally saved my life. I am certain it saved our organization. We were becoming less effective as we took on more and more. By scaling back, focusing, and committing to our most effective programs, we increased the level of our performance significantly.

A Personal Practice

Complete the following sentences:

1. When I feel most alive I am... _____
   _____
   _____

2. My friends keep telling me I need to... _____
   _____
   _____

3. Sometimes I am afraid God thinks... _____
   _____
   _____

4. When I was little I wanted to... _____
   _____
   _____

5. I wish the world was more... _____
   _____
   _____

6. My heart aches when... _____
   _____
   _____

7. I am inspired by... _____
   _____
   _____

8. When I am at my best, people tell me... _____
   _____
   _____

9. I am most at ease when... _____
   _____
   _____

10. My greatest dream is... _____
_____
_____

Okay, that last one might be hard. Now, look over your responses and notice the points where your personal experiences and feelings are aligned with what you wish for the world. Do you see connections to what you are already doing and what you wish to see in the world? This is the meeting point of your personal and professional missions.

A Congregational Practice

Let's work together to draft a liturgy that best describes your understanding of God and our relationship to God and one another. Maybe, like Friendship Presbyterian Church, it's a new edition of the Lord's Prayer. Maybe it's more of a creed. Maybe it's a poem or a rap or a video. The content can be shaped by the genre, or the other way around.

Whatever you are writing/imagining, use real language. Don't use inaccessible words that people have to look up to find out what they mean. Tell what you think about God in a way that touches the heart and inspires the imagination. Be playful and have fun.

Small Group Discussion Questions

1. How do your own values align with the church's values?

2. What are your church's vision and mission statements? Do they inspire you? Are they honest? Are they clear?

3. Does your church use its technological systems (database, email, website, social media) efficiently? How could you improve?

4. What opportunities are before the church right now that could be distractions more than additions? Does the Spinout Checklist apply?

---

[1] https://www.usatoday.com/story/money/cars/2013/06/09/ford-f150-built-ford-tough-tag-line-advertising/2402587/

Chapter Seven

Funding Your Flying Habit

Checklist

- ❒ Assess your savings, credit score, and banking relationships
- ❒ Develop a budget for your level of flying and your burn rate
- ❒ Shop around for good deals on safe planes and instructors
- ❒ As you take off, watch the $20 bills fly out of your tailpipe

*"If the Wright brothers were alive today Wilbur would have to fire
Orville to reduce costs."*
—Herb Kelleher, pilot for Southwest Airlines

My day had gone like any other in my short twelve-year-old life. I got up that morning, fixed breakfast, caught the bus to school, attended class, and took the bus home. When I walked in the door to my kitchen that afternoon, I knew something was wrong. Both of my parents were home. They were never home early.

I looked at my mother with a question in my eyes. "What's going on?" I asked. I was barely breathing. She looked defeated. Whatever had happened hurt my mom, and my protective instincts rose up ready to do battle with whatever or whoever had hurt her. She said the words slowly, or maybe it was just that time seemed to slow down for me to catch up. She said, "We were both laid off from the company." I looked through the kitchen to the dining room table where I saw my stepfather's nameplate that had sat on his desk at his office for the past ten years sitting in a box.

My mind was racing: *What does this mean? What is going to happen next? What can I do to help?*

Maybe you have experienced this moment—the moment when the security of the life you once knew drops from beneath you suddenly. You find yourself standing in your kitchen, disoriented, trying to imagine reinventing yourself, your life, your sense of security—all this, with the paralyzing pressure of a mortgage payment due in 15 days. Our family, like so many today, didn't have savings to pull us through. We didn't have the "rainy day fund" that cushions the collapse. We were in full crisis.

What we did have was a strong extended family ready to help, and a "do what you have to do" attitude that pushed my mom to take a temporary job at a department store selling tree ornaments that holiday season. She then took a job with a recruiting company, and then worked for a local nonprofit. My father started his own construction company, though business was painfully slow. We made it through in large part because of their courage, but we all have the scars to prove it.

I started my journey to financial independence that day I watched my parents deal with their layoffs. I didn't want to be a burden on anyone else, and I wanted to help others as I could. I would never be owned by or indebted to another person. I would never be vulnerable to that kind of crisis. I would work myself to death if necessary to be sure I never lived through that pain again.

For many people, this experience makes them fear-based and fiscally conservative. They hoard money, scared that, should they need it, they better have it saved up. I learned that lesson, but it never served me well. It made me feel small and scared and stingy. I felt like I couldn't breathe. So, I flipped the message. I decided to live with this story about money: Money is energy, an exchange between people that represents trade and investment. Money comes and goes. I will always have enough. I am more resourceful than I know. When forced into a scary space, I can draw on energy, opportunities, and people who open new possibilities. People of good will want me to succeed, just as I want that for them. I just have to keep moving, trusting, and loving.

When I flipped my story about money, I realized that both stories could be true. One felt more life-giving, and one more life-taking. One helped me live more fully; one made me hesitate and feel vulnerable. I had the power to choose which one had influence in my life. It became a literal exercise in mind over matter.

Let me hasten to say that I am a white, educated woman who has more economic opportunities that many of my friends of color. I absolutely see and acknowledge that privilege. I spend significant life energy working to eradicate that injustice. I also believe my lessons are still true. No matter what your situation, you have access to energy, opportunities, and people who can help you gain access to the resources you need. I believe that is the way God designed the world to work.

Your Money Story

What about you? What are the earliest lessons you learned about money that influence how you live today? In the interviews I have completed with church leaders, I've heard reflections such as:

"My parents fought all the time about money. I don't want to talk about it at all with my partner. I just let him handle it."

"We had plenty of money growing up. I could have anything I wanted. Looking back, I regret that. It took me a long time to understand the value of money and that a lot of people were not as lucky as I was."

"We used to use food stamps. We didn't have money. But I don't remember thinking we were poor. My mom made sure we had what we needed, and we were a close family. It's only in looking back that I realize how creative she was. I can't imagine the stress she must have felt."

"I make a good salary today and have plenty of money, but I still feel panic that I will lose my job and end up on the streets. I know in my head that won't happen, but something deep in me still carries that fear."

Every one of us has a money story. Most of us haven't chosen our story. Ours was given to us by our experiences as children watching our parents or other adults in our lives navigate their own stories. We learned by watching and experiencing. The stories root themselves deeply within us and impact everything. The good news is that, as adults, we now have control over the role we allow these stories to play in our lives. Better yet, we can rewrite them as needed when they aren't serving us well.

Let's try this together. Grab a piece of paper and pen. Or, open your laptop/tablet to a new document.

1. Think back to your childhood and write down what you learned about money from watching your parents.

2. When you first had control of your own money, maybe after graduating from high school, how did you relate to it? Did you spend it all? Did you spend that and more, running up debt? Did you save every penny you could?

3. Did your early relationship with your money reflect what you saw growing up, or did you establish a new relationship with your money?

4. What would you do differently if you could rewrite your money story?

Now, I want you to do just that using an exercise that I first learned from author Martha Beck in one of her coaching trainings.[1] Imagine that "Money" is a living being. Maybe it's another person. Maybe it's an animal. Take out a new piece of paper, and write a kind letter to Money. Realize that Money is an innocent energy that loves to play and help people. Here are the things you should include in your letter.

a. Tell Money what you *really* think of it. Be totally honest.

b. Apologize to Money for all the negative things you think about it and all the mean things you said about it behind its back.

c. Apologize as well for the times you've grasped Money so hard you hurt it, clinging with talons of desperation that nearly choked it to death.

d. Also apologize for times you've been ungrateful to Money: times when it was there for you—as much as it could be—and all you did was complain about how it wasn't doing enough.

e. Tell Money that you release it from your anxiety and anger. See it as a creature, an animal that wants to play and love and reproduce.

f. Offer as much affection as you can. Tell Money it's done no harm (in and of itself) and that you forgive it for all the ways humans misuse it.

g. Invite Money to come play with you. Try to feel the joy of hosting it in your life, of giving it a place to be safe and warm and dry.

h. Let it know it can come to you anytime it wants, in any way it wants.

Now pretend you *are* Money, and write a letter back to yourself. Tell yourself (writing *as* Money)...

a. ...why Money may be avoiding you (write this as "I, Money, am avoiding you because...").

b. ...why Money wants to come to you ("I, Money, want to come to you because...").

c. ...what you could do to invite it in ("I, Money, would love it if you would...").

d. ...what you could do to make life more fun for you and your money ("I, Money, would love to have fun with you doing...").

After you have completed these exercises, just sit back and watch what happens in your life, your organization, or your church. Your energy around money will be different. As your energy shifts, so too does the role money plays in your life.

Why Start Here?

Why would I have you spend this much time on your personal money story? Because it always impacts your *congregational* money story. Every. Single. Time. If you are part of the budgeting process of your church and you grew up eating food from the local food shelter, there is a strong chance that your budgets are fiscally conservative. If you grew up never knowing where money came from, but there was plenty to go around, you might be more comfortable with unbalanced budgets in which you hope that giving makes up for the shortfalls. When you are working as a team to shape the financial future of your church, you will run into these stories operating in the background. Make them transparent and then you will understand why Bob always defends not spending anything from the endowment, or why Sarah wants to see the financial reports every single month, or why Jim won't sign off of that second equity loan to pay the salary for the new associate. Our public fiscal leadership is shaped profoundly by our personal money experiences. Once we know them, we work better as a team.

Jesus knew this too. He talked about money *all the time*. Sixteen of his thirty-eight parables talk about how to handle money and possessions. One out of ten verses (288 in all) in the gospels deals directly with money. The Bible offers 500 verses on prayer, less than 500 verses on faith, but more than 2,000 verses on money and possessions.[2] Clearly, humans have always struggled to believe that we are enough, and we will have enough. We need only be creative.

The Crash Is Real

Today, most mainline congregations in the United States are struggling to make ends meet. None of us is surprised. People don't come to church as often, and they don't give as much. Do that math, and you realize that if your church depends on Sunday giving as its primary income source, you're in trouble. It's even worse, because most of churches' big givers are older members, and they are...*how shall I say this delicately?*...dying. At the moment, some churches are benefiting from planned giving donations from these older members, which are often outlined in their wills. But once this generation passes on, we are looking at an entirely new reality for how we fund ministry going forward.

I could write an entire book on the financial collapse and possible financial rebirth of the mainline church in North America. It's not unlike what we are seeing in other industries: publishing, higher education, fabric manufacturing, car sales, malls, office supply stores, bookstores, sound recording studios, and video rental stores/boxes.[3] Each of these industries and the individual franchises within them must decide if they are going to pivot or die. We are no different.

Instead of moaning about what used to work, let's look at some of the new models and tools now available to congregations that might help you envision a financial future with multiple funding streams. I should be honest: some of the institutional trappings that we have enjoyed may be unsustainable going forward. Every church may not be able to afford a fulltime clergy person. Some churches will need to sell their buildings. Others may have to consider merging with another congregation and pooling resources. These steps are part of the financial deconstruction phase we are seeing right now in many congregations and denominations. Once we get on the other side of this, we will see a new world of possibility. It's that world that has to be convinced that our best days will be ahead.

Emerging Funding Tools

We are lucky. We are living in the most creative, innovative age in human history. We have more ideas, resources, partners, programs, and tools available to us today than ever before. We are also living in the most disruptive time in modern history, during which the institutions we once counted on to shape our society are being disrupted by entrepreneurial innovators who are using technology to offer consumers more access to more tools every day.

You have access to these tools as you frame your future financial model for your congregation. Because we also already know that we can't depend on Sunday giving as the main revenue generator, we need to begin accessing other sources of funding to power our ministries. Here are a few:

- **Incubators:** Incubators support new ministries or those at the beginning of their start-up phase by providing services such as mentoring, management training, or office space. They support new ministry leaders by putting them into an environment rich with collaboration and mentorship as the new ministry finds its way to a sustainable model. Incubators do not typically involve direct financial support; instead, the support comes from the in-kind investments of the other incubator members.

- **Accelerators:** An accelerator works with ministry startups for a short and specific amount of time, usually from three to four months, to sharpen the funding model and connect the leaders to future donors/investors. Accelerators also offer startups a specific amount of capital, usually somewhere around $20,000. In exchange for capital and guidance, accelerators usually require some financial return on investment, such as an apportionment or tithe back to the accelerator organization.

- **Angel Investors:** Instead of the concept of the "shark tank," made popular by the similarly named television show, angel investors for ministry projects are building what many refer to as the "dolphin tank," a much more supportive environment of investors committed to your ministry's success. Made up of individuals and organizations, these investors shape agreements that require the funded project to "pay it forward" after a period of time to support another ministry in need of funding support.

- **Denominational Loan Funds:** Most denominational loan funds today have more money than ever before and have changed their bylaws to allow them the freedom to invest in a wider range of projects than in the past. Most denomination loan funds can now fund projects across denominations, instead of just in their own. These loans are typically low interest, but do have the same security requirements of a typical bank loan.

- **Crowdfunding:** Crowdfunding is a strategic tool for short-term projects—such as raising funds for a youth mission trip or a local community building project. Crowdfunding is built on a "campaign" mindset, in which you run a campaign for a specific period of time to raise the funds needed. Fees to use these platforms range from between 2–6 percent per transaction. The typical campaign raises an average of $5,000 in total.

- **Product Platforms:** Etsy is one of the most popular sales platforms. Congregational members may design arts projects (ornaments, scarves, t-shirts, etc.), and sell these products through an online store. A church in Philadelphia sells knitted scarves online to support their homeless ministry. Many congregations use these proceeds to support programs in their church.

- **Campus Conversion:** More and more churches are transforming their buildings and campuses into multiuse rentable facilities used seven days a week by various organizations. The church receives rental income and becomes a community hub for local business and other NGO activities. A church in Washington, D.C., redesigned their campus into a multi-story shopping center, while retaining the use of the top floor for their church activities. The rest of the space is used for retail, generating enough income to fund their entire congregational budget.

You will be able to add to this list based on resources available in your community. The point is to be creative about the new tools out there. Because we know that sustaining ministry will require a combination of funding sources going forward, now is the time to get creative about options worthy of your exploration.

Emerging Funding Models

Funding your ministry into the future is going to depend a great deal of the kind of model you adopt for revenue generation. One of the byproducts of the "entrepreneurial age" is that every time we turn around, someone has created a new model for making money. As long as it's congruent with our ministry's values, we would be wise to learn from it.

Here are some new models I see congregations embracing today:

The Affiliate Model

Some churches develop exciting partnerships with other organizations or businesses, which add value to both organizations. For example, sometimes churches partner with well-known universities to host a lecture series for the community. Sometimes they might partner together to appeal for donor money to support the shared community project. At the core of this model is the understanding: "Your success is our success: we benefit each other by our affiliation with each other."

Countryside Community Church in Omaha, Nebraska, is affiliated with an exciting project called the Tri-Faith Initiative. The Tri-Faith Initiative is an intentionally multi-faith campus. Built on 33 acres, it's made up of three Abrahamic faith groups who have chosen to be in relationship together as neighbors on one campus, committed to practicing respect, acceptance, and trust. Their three members are of the Jewish, Christian, and Islamic faiths: Temple Israel, Countryside Community Church (UCC), and The American Muslim Institute (formerly the American Institute of Islamic Studies and Culture). Together, they formed a 501c3 to raise money for the project. Individually, they also raised money for their congregations by telling the story of this exciting affiliation. This created four exceptional fund-raising streams through their shared fund and their individual funds, generating millions of dollars in making this campus the reality.

The Center for Applied Wisdom is an exciting program affiliated with San Francisco Theological Seminary and Stanford University. Their mission is to bring together wisdom and spirituality through work with social visionaries to ignite sustainable change. If they had tried to raise funds on their own, they might have been hindered by their "faith-based" emphasis.

Instead, because of their affiliated partnerships, particularly with Stanford University, they won a grant through the Google Foundation to build this center benefiting all of the partners.

Questions to consider:

1. What strong partnerships could you build that open affiliate opportunities to your ministry?

2. What qualities are you seeking in a partner? What do you hope to gain from this partnership, beyond financial aid, and what do you have to offer in return?

The Barter Model

The barter model involves the sharing of ministry resources between people or other organizations without money being directly exchanged. Both partners are actively engaged in the value creation process. You've experienced this when going to the doctor. As you're leaving, the doctor or nurse might hand you a sample pack of prescription medication for you to try. They're working in partnership with the pharmaceutical industry to see which drugs are the most popular with patients...and, one hopes, the most effective.

The roots of bartering run deep in the Christian tradition. Acts 4:32–35 tells us the story of the early church members sharing everything they had. We moved away from that practice as our tradition matured and we accumulated more wealth in our systems. Today, as we watch the deconstruction of our denominations, bartering between congregations makes more sense.

Linden Hills United Church of Christ in Minneapolis, Minnesota, barters for their youth ministry. They realized many years ago that they didn't have the capacity in-house to offer a compelling youth ministry, but other churches in the area could do that. Together with a number of other congregations, they created a nonprofit that leans into the gifts of each member congregation to support community-wide youth ministry. Linden Hills UCC sends their youth to this program. Other churches offer staff time to the programs. Other churches offer their space. By working together and trading resources, they've been able to provide a life-giving ministry to young people in their community.

Just down the road from Linden Hills is another interesting ministry called the Springhouse Ministry Center. It's a beautiful building in the Salem neighborhood that houses three partnership ministries: First Christian Church (Disciples of Christ), Salem English Lutheran Church, and Lyndale United Church of Christ. Each congregation worships in its own way, and together they share common ministries such as education and mission. By sharing the building together, they free up resources for their community ministries.

Questions to consider:

1. Is there a mutual interest in the relationship that would eliminate any sense of competition?

2. Will our brands get confused by being associated with each other?

3. Are our cultures compatible?

The Cross-Supporting Model

The cross-supporting model offers complimentary "services" beyond the core ministries, with the aim of deepening engagement with the existing community. For people in the congregation, they benefit by having access to more services, such as healthcare, loans, credit union bank accounts, childcare, K-12 education, legal support, etc., at a lower cost. The church is strengthened because most of these services can be underwritten by government/community grants, individual donations, or fees for service profit-sharing.

The cross-supporting model holds the most potential for its ease of entry for congregations and their members. The options for complementary programs and services are endless. The key is negotiating a financial model that benefits the congregation, its members, and the service provider.

While City of Refuge UCC should be known for many innovations in congregational life, they are a great example of cross-supporting ministries that sustain the congregation and make a difference in the wider community. Within the building that houses the worship center for the congregation, you will also find a medical clinic funded by community and government grants there to support those in need. You will also walk past a row of offices which house the union organizations that fight for workers' rights and fair employment. You will pass classrooms that offer theological training for adults who want access to seminary level training but can't afford it. This last program, called Project Access, is funded through student tuition, grants, and donations.

Denominations also provide cross-supporting models for supporting member sustainability. In 2015, the Evangelical Lutheran Church of America launched a credit union available to any ELCA member in their churches across the nation. Doing this was a brilliant move because it added tangible value to being a member of any ELCA church across the country. Other denominations have also set up Amazon Smile accounts for members to use. When a person purchases a product on Amazon, a percentage of that purchase goes back to the denominational body.

Questions to consider:

1. Can the services be bundled in ways that generate new revenue streams for the congregation while also providing world-class service to the members?

2. Is there a natural need for expanded services in your area? Would offering them make life better for the people living in your community?

I don't intend this to be an exhaustive list.[4] You would die reading it. What I hope you are seeing is that we live in an age with so many creative options. I have a motto that I live by: "You can always have your way if you have enough ways." When it comes to funding your ministries, you just need to discover enough ways.

A Personal Practice

Personal Money Motivation Assessment

Listed below are questions to help you clarify your relationship to money and the influence it has over your life. Circle the number that most closely corresponds to your feelings on each scale.

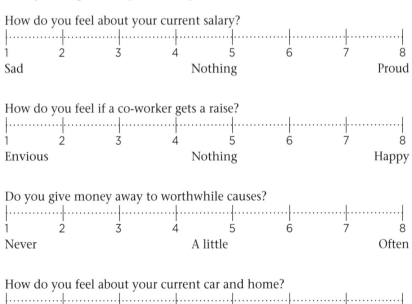

How do you feel about your current salary?

```
|..........|..........|..........|..........|..........|..........|..........|
1          2          3          4          5          6          7          8
Sad                              Nothing                          Proud
```

How do you feel if a co-worker gets a raise?

```
|..........|..........|..........|..........|..........|..........|..........|
1          2          3          4          5          6          7          8
Envious                          Nothing                          Happy
```

Do you give money away to worthwhile causes?

```
|..........|..........|..........|..........|..........|..........|..........|
1          2          3          4          5          6          7          8
Never                            A little                         Often
```

How do you feel about your current car and home?

```
|..........|..........|..........|..........|..........|..........|..........|
1          2          3          4          5          6          7          8
I can do better                  Nothing                          Proud
```

When you want to buy something expensive, you

1	2	3	4	5	6	7	8
Say you can't afford it			Ignore it				Buy it

Do you feel money is evil?

1	2	3	4	5	6	7	8
Yes			Not sure				No

What is the meaning you give money?

1	2	3	4	5	6	7	8
Necessary Evil			None				Useful Tool

If you had all of the money in the world that you wanted, what would you do?

1	2	3	4	5	6	7	8
No idea			What I am doing now				Change my life

Do you feel wealthy now?

1	2	3	4	5	6	7	8
No			Not sure				Yes

What did your parents think about money?

1	2	3	4	5	6	7	8
Fought over it			Not sure				Not a problem

What are your thoughts generally about money?

1	2	3	4	5	6	7	8
Worry about it			It depends				Positive

Do you have enough saved if you lost your job and needed to cover 3 months of living expenses?

1	2	3	4	5	6	7	8
No			Not sure				Yes

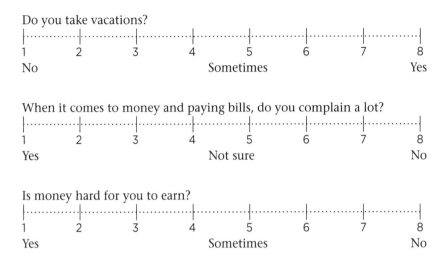

Do you take vacations?

```
|··············|··············|··············|··············|··············|··············|··············|
1              2              3              4              5              6              7              8
No                                          Sometimes                                                Yes
```

When it comes to money and paying bills, do you complain a lot?

```
|··············|··············|··············|··············|··············|··············|··············|
1              2              3              4              5              6              7              8
Yes                                         Not sure                                                  No
```

Is money hard for you to earn?

```
|··············|··············|··············|··············|··············|··············|··············|
1              2              3              4              5              6              7              8
Yes                                         Sometimes                                                 No
```

Add up the numbers and tally your score: _____

- *If you scored between 15 and 45, you likely struggle with your feelings about money. Money is a challenging topic and one that makes you feel anxious and scared. Your opportunity is in changing the story you are telling yourself about the role money plays in your life. You need to recognize that money is value-neutral. What story can you write about your financial life that gives you more power and agency?*

- *If you scored between 46 and 90, you may find yourself "agnostic" about money. You don't get triggered by it, but you also aren't leveraging it fully in your life. You have the opportunity to explore what difference money can make in your life and what good you could do by giving money away. Money can be a powerful tool in creating a more just world for all.*

- *If you scored between 91 and 120, you have a powerful internal story about money as a tool for good in your life and the world. You are not afraid of money and not anxious about the role it plays in your life. Keep doing what you are doing, and teach the rest of us!*

A Congregational Practice

In small groups or with the church council leaders, write down your congregation's money story. You can use the questions listed in this chapter to guide your narrative. Think about the times the congregation had plenty of money, and the times that were lean. How did the leaders make decisions? How did you all set priorities? Who was left out? How would you rewrite the story if you could do it again? What would you change?

Now, write the story you want future generations to tell. What lessons do you want them to learn? What values do you hope they carry forward? What kind of church do you hope exists for them to lead forward?

Is there a gap?

Small Group Discussion Questions

1. How do you feel about your church's financial future? Are you anxious? Proud? Confused?

2. If your church had unlimited money, what would change? What would you do differently?

3. Are you all comfortable talking about money? Why or why not?

4. Are you doing what needs to be done to be creative about the church's financial future? What more could you be doing?

5. How much of your church's giving comes from people 70 years old and older?

---

[1] https://www.facebook.com/events/783292968538774/

[2] https://www.preachingtoday.com/illustrations/1996/december/410.html

[3] https://www.usatoday.com/story/money/economy/2017/12/28/americas-25-dying-industries-include-sound-studios-textiles-newspapers/982514001/

[4] If you want to know more about emerging funding models for ministry, download my e-book, "Financial Models for Your Ministry," from http://www.progressiverenewal.org.

Chapter Eight

Managing "Comms"

"Ask any pilot how they started flying and you will hear a love story."
Captain Eric Auxier, US Airline Pilot

We have two wonderful friends named Brian and Joyce. Both of them grew up in Mormon families in Utah. Joyce's family, while claiming the title "Mormon," were not particularly orthodox in their practice. Brian's family was the opposite. When a boy raised in the Mormon faith turns 18, usually he is sent on a two-year mission trip to convert people to Mormonism. In Brian's case, he was sent to Japan, a primarily secular culture. Can you imagine? Brian tells a funny story about his experience there:

> The basic story of Mormonism is that a man named Joseph Smith was approached by two angelic beings with a revelation from God. In Japanese, the word for angelic person is ningen. But the word for carrot is ninjin. They are very close to one another, especially when spoken.

You can imagine these white Mormon missionary men coming to Japan to convert these people, and when they say "angelic" in their thick accents, it came out sounding like "carrots." So I kept running into all these Japanese people who thought that two carrots descended from on high with a great revelation from God.

Ah, the joys of "evangelizing"! If you have ever played a game of "telephone," you realize that what we say and what someone else hears can easily get confused. If that confusion is unchecked, we can end up acting on really bad information. This might be hysterically funny when we play a game of "telephone," but could have more serious consequences when we are coordinating planes flying through the air. Given the speed at which we are living, miscommunication is more the norm than the exception.

Your Controls, My Controls

Communication is paramount when flying. You don't want confusion in the cockpit, especially about who is flying the plane. Early in your training you learn about the "positive exchange of controls." It's always assumed that the pilot sitting in the left seat is the captain and is directing the flight. In most circumstances, the captain taxis the plane to the runway to begin the flight. But the captain can then hand over the controls of the plane to the first officer by using a standardized phrase that all pilots recognize. She will say to her first officer or fellow pilot, "Your controls." She remains in control of the plane until she hears him say back, "My controls," and then visually verifies that he does, in fact, have his hands on the yoke and feet on the rudder pedals. Then she repeats back her acknowledgment, "Your controls," and releases her hands and feet from the inputs. This call-and-response pattern ensures that command of the plane is safely transferred between the two pilots.

Teamwork can be an elegant dance when we know what to expect and can anticipate the calls likely to come our way. The aviation world quickly figured out that we needed an efficient and clear system for communicating, because it can't afford distraction or confusion in the cockpit. That is how people die. The church could learn from this.

While we are not in danger of falling from the sky or hitting the side of a mountain, when we are not communicating clearly with our colleagues and church members, we are using costly energy and setting ourselves up for misrepresentation, miscommunication, and ineffective leadership. Granted, it would be weird to use aviation speak in our daily interactions.

Me: *Chris, Cameron here.*

Chris: *Go ahead, Cameron.*

Me: *In my office, settled in until 3:00 p.m., working on my sermon.*

Chris: *Roger, Cameron. I am in my office until 4:00 p.m. PT. Expect conversation about the Sunday service at 10:45 a.m. ET. Lunch will be at noon.*

Me: *Roger. Expect conversation at 10:45 a.m. Lunch at noon. Cameron out.*

Actually, as I am writing this, it's oddly appealing. It's clear. It's concise. Okay...it's still weird. Flying, of course, is a more controlled environment than church would be. But I am shocked at the number of times and ways we miscommunicate between each other.

I was working with a church in Madison, Wisconsin, via a video conference one night. They are the typical case study in mainline church today. They were founded in 1951 at the height of the church growth era. Today, they are an aging congregation with grey-haired saints abounding, their facilities in need of repair, their budget declining year after year, and they would do almost anything to get families with young kids to attend. On the call that night, we were struggling with our WIFI connection. My voice and picture kept coming in and out. I was giving an update on the results of an online assessment that we had completed for them. We were just at the section about how the congregation handled conflict when they heard me say, "This church shows a...level of conflict and a...to handle conflict in healthy ways." I didn't realize that my transmission had frozen at those moments on their end. When we finally reconnected, I found myself in a free-for-all of total panic by the lay leaders. They couldn't believe it! They felt as if everything was going so well at the church. How could there be people reporting conflict? Were they completely out of touch with what was happening at the church? What was going on? This was terrible news!

I was dumbfounded. Then I realized the problem: they had missed critical words in my verbal report. What I said was, "This church shows a low level of conflict and a strong ability to handle conflict in healthy ways." They heard the opposite, filling in the gaps with their fears of what I might say. You can imagine the damage that could have resulted had we not corrected that miscommunication. As I told the group, "This is how nasty rumors get started!"

The Power of Aligned Communication

Last year I was working with an organization that had just hired a new CEO. We were together on a retreat where I was facilitating their strategic alignment conversation. We designed a process through which everyone contributed their perspectives on what the priorities should be for the coming year, and then we narrowed those priorities down to four main ones that the group could embrace.

During that narrowing process, we noticed that one member of the team was increasingly agitated. She was a senior executive in the system, and her body language suggested that she was uncomfortable with the direction of the conversation. Other members of the team, noticing her obvious signals, begin reaching out to engage her in the hopes that they could better understand her concerns. Instead of engaging their offer, she withdrew even further. When I asked the group to take the four priorities and narrow them even further to a single statement, the rest of the group readily agreed and got busy. The senior executive, however, sat with her arms crossed alone on the sofa. Again, her team members reached out to her, asking for her to contribute to the work they were creating together. She continued to refuse. At that point, I entered into the space to try to make transparent her competing commitments and agenda.

"Can you help your team understand why this conversation feels uncomfortable to you?" I asked.

"I don't know. It just does," she said.

"Your teammates have crafted a draft of a statement that has an impact on your collective work. It seems like that statement doesn't include things that are important to you. Can you help them understand what is missing?" I asked.

"I don't have their statement in front of me, so I can't respond to that," she said. "I will give my feedback when I have had time to think about all of this."

At this point, we were at a turning point in the conversation. Had I given her permission to delay feedback, her objections could have undermined the goal of our current conversation. Our commitment in that retreat was to contribute in real time to the collective goals of the group. Her delaying tactic, apart from being bad behavior, violated the integrity of the space we had generated for this creative process.

We sat in silence.

Then one member of the group got up and handed her computer to the senior executive, saying, *"Here's the statement. We would really value any ways that you could strengthen and improve it."*

At that point, she angrily pushed the computer back at the woman and stormed out of the room.

We sat in silence.

Then another senior executive on the team spoke up and said, *"I just realized that she doesn't have the same things at stake in this conversation and therefore isn't as committed to our goals of having it in the first place. I'm glad that's clear now. It seems like we can move forward more quickly."* And they did. That senior executive who stormed out of that meeting was not with the organization two weeks later.

What happened?

We began that conversation with twelve different people, with different agendas and commitments, in the room. They shared a "given state" in common: they were employed by the same organization and held to the same, intersecting performance goals. What we had to carefully architect while we were together was a "generated state," in which our trust in one another, our intention in the conversation, and our goals created an environment in which breakthrough thinking was possible (though not guaranteed). It wasn't enough that we were together in a room and joined by the common thread of employment. It was important that we generated a field of trust strong enough to hold competing agendas until we gained alignment.

Our alignment came through being able to hold space for the honest reality of our misalignment, oddly enough. We could stand the silence because we knew it was generating the liminal space needed for deepening the conversation.

Think of it this way: imagine a sound wave with its peaks and valleys.

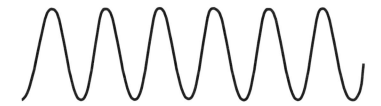

This might represent the state of a conversation that is in alignment—people are aligned in their commitments, agendas, and goals. But this rarely happens in the beginning. We usually have hidden, conflicting, or competing commitments, agendas, and goals. That looks something like this:

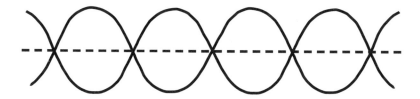

Here, you literally have noise cancellation or productivity cancellation. Our hidden, conflicting, or competing commitments, agendas, and goals are canceling out our contributions. This happens to so many teams in organizations and companies. They are not productive or produce poor quality products/services because they are stuck in this diminished, canceling pattern. But leadership is bringing *alignment* (which is different than *consensus*) to the conversation so that forward progress can be made. To do that, you have to expose the places of misalignment. That can happen any number of ways. In the example above, we used the pattern of "silence-reflection-silence" to push forward.

What I have learned is that, if you can hold the space long enough, the group will lead you to the misaligned places. Once you are there, you can begin the work of establishing alignment. When that is established, magic happens. You get amplification leading to peak performance and breakthroughs!

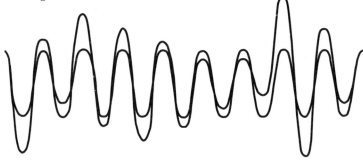

When you finally get to this point, you are ready to say "yes" to the work you are to do together in the world. The work will be ready to be done. Most importantly, the field needed to establish the work will have integrity and be worthy of your team's highest and best efforts.

Set the Tone

Sticking with the sound wave analogy, your job as a leader is to set the melody, the single line of music that anchors the rest of the song your congregation is playing. Have you ever heard a song without a melody line? If you have, you probably don't remember it. It's the melody that sticks in our minds and makes us fall in love with the song. Everything else builds from there. You set the melody line so that everyone else knows how to harmonize.

When I step into a cockpit as pilot-in-command, my copilot is looking to me to set expectations for how I will "play" that environment. He looks to me to determine how "by the book" I will be (and expect him to be). If I am critical of him or harsh in my critiques, he might hesitate to tell me when he sees something amiss. If I ignore him, he might do his work without coordinating with me. Your team needs to know your expectations. They need to know what behaviors are appreciated and what behaviors are not. They need to know that they are supported and valued.

My friend Phoenix was struggling with her staff team. Her team members, who had worked together for years, were engaging in petty fights that had eroded trust within the team. They were undisciplined in their working environment. Soon, this behavior would spill into the relationships with their partners. She needed to intervene. While she was clear about the vision and mission of the organization, she realized that she also needed to be clear about the culture she expected in the office environment. She called a meeting with her team. As they sat around the table looking expectantly at her, she squared her shoulders, looked each of them in the eyes, and said:

In a professional environment, staff members are competent, respectful, accountable, mature, and take their work seriously.

In a professional environment, staff members dress appropriately, show up on time for meetings, are pleasant and polite (even to persons who are irritating), are reliable, are helpful, take initiative, challenge themselves, and are willing to learn.

In a professional environment, staff members don't lie, bully, gossip, cheat, share information that should not be shared, form cliques, or lose their tempers.

In a professional environment, staff members alert their supervisor when things are going off-track; take responsibility for—and alert their supervisor to—mistakes; recognize that feedback (even critical feedback) is part of the job and is not personal so they don't get defensive; write clearly and professionally; meet deadlines consistently; demonstrate a willingness to be flexible when the organization is trying to achieve certain goals; and look around and see areas for improvement instead of looking around and seeing problems.

In a professional work environment, staff members work with their office doors open (unless on a call or working to meet an intense deadline and, if either is the case, letting folks know with a post to Slack).

In a professional work environment, staff members consistently demonstrate collegiality, practice civil discourse, follow HR policies like requesting vacation in a timely manner and prior to the desired time off, and contacting your supervisor by email or phone if you are sick and unable to be in the office.

I need to be clear about this. I expect a professional work environment. Any questions?

They sat in stunned silence. Then the most remarkable thing happened: they agreed that they needed to change and committed to make it so. As the leader in this space, Phoenix set a new tone. She was clear about her expectations. She set clear boundaries. No one questioned that she meant every word. Today, they are a stronger team because Phoenix had the wisdom, courage, and commitment to lead.

Would You Care to Make a Comment?

I was working with Morgan, a pastor in Baltimore, when the riots in support of the #BlackLivesMatter movement erupted in the city. That morning, he got a call from the local news station asking if he would be willing to come in for an interview. He would be on a panel with another pastor—an older white man, from the conservative Evangelical church in the community. He panicked. This guy was known for being ruthless and was always crystal clear on his talking points. Even if he wasn't, he would be given more credibility just because he was an older white man, while Morgan was a thirty-two-year-old African American man.

He called me looking for someone to help him get prepped. Luckily for me, I have had the privilege of working with one of the best in the business, Macky Alston at Auburn Seminary, who taught me a model for just these moments. I remember my training with Macky: He drew a triangle on a piece of paper. In the middle of the triangle, I was to write my core message, the *one thing* I wanted people to remember out of everything I said. Then he moved to the points of the triangle. "The first point," he said, "are the statistics you can name to support your core message. If you want to tell me that homelessness is growing, be ready with the stats to support that." Then, for the second point on the triangle, he said, "Here is a story that you will tell that pulls at my heart strings or is memorable in some way. Tell me about the homeless person you talked to last week or the way you daughter cried when she realized that not everyone has a bed to sleep in. Don't make up a story. Don't lie. But find a story that touches me." Then he pointed at the final point on the triangle and said, "This is where you list the scriptures that support your core message. What did Jesus say about homelessness? Be ready to reference the verses." It came out looking like this:

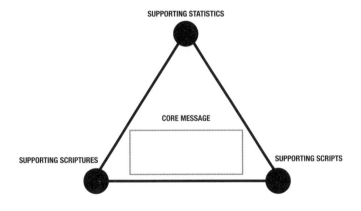

Macky went on: "When you are in front of a camera, the name of the game is to state your core message as many times as possible. The panelist or interviewer may try to distract you. That's okay, just pivot to your story and then back to your core message, or pivot to a scripture and back to your core message. Never let them get you away from your message." Many of us in this world of national religious leadership are indebted to Macky Alston for his wisdom and commitment to preparing us to lead.

Morgan hadn't been trained by Macky and needed help immediately. I reviewed the messaging strategy model with him and then we got to work nailing down his core message and supporting points. Then I drilled him.

> **Me:** *"Morgan, what do you make of all of these people flooding our streets as a part of this protest? It seems your church is at the heart of helping to organize some of it."*
>
> **Morgan:** *"We believe that the killing of innocent black men and women is a problem in this country and must stop. Jesus commanded us to love our neighbors, to treat others as we would want to be treated, and we are simply calling for fair treatment under the law."*
>
> **Me:** *"Don't you think there are better ways to get fair treatment than risking destruction to property and clogging our streets?"*
>
> **Morgan:** *"No one wants to be marching in the streets tonight. We would all like to be at home with our families. But we believe that the killing of innocent black men and women is a problem in this country and must stop. Police killed 1,147 people in 2017. Black people were 25 percent of those killed despite being only 13 percent of the population.[1]"*

Morgan and I went over and over his points until they were seared into his brain. When he went on the news station that night, I am proud to say that he nailed the interview, giving us all one of the refreshingly few examples of public Christian leaders speaking truth to power. I was inspired beyond words.

I would strongly encourage you, pastor and lay leader alike, to get in the practice of developing messaging strategies even if you never use them on the nightly news. Sadly, we may see a day when a crisis breaks out in your community, and you need to step up to the camera or talk to a reporter on the phone. More than that, the messaging strategy model instills a discipline in your thinking about issues that are often complicated and hard to talk about. I have used messaging strategies to draft sermons, speeches, blog posts, responses to critics via email, and devotions. Get in the practice of creating them. Keep them in a file on your computer, ready to use whenever you need them. If and when you are put on the spot to make a public statement, you will be glad you did.

Talking to Your Wider Community

Ideally, you have a more developed communication strategy that just communicating with your members and hoping a reporter calls you. You would be wise to use all of your tools. Today we have more free and low cost communication tools than ever before. The trick is figuring out which are the right tools for the right audience and the right message. Let's look at the main ones you are likely to use:

Website

Your website is your front door for new people interested in your church. You have to have one. But it also needs to represent you well. If your website was last updated in 2007, you need to stop reading this and go hire someone to build you a new site. I am not a fan of letting a member design your site. It's such an essential part of your communication toolbox that I recommend you let a professional help you design it. Most sites are built using WordPress or Squarespace. Stick to one of those. Please, I beg you, don't use clip art. Ever.

Email

MailChimp and Constant Contact are the most popular email marketing platforms that churches use. They both have great pricing for nonprofits, and easy-to-use email design interfaces. They also allow you to segment your audiences and run campaigns over time to develop those audiences. Both of these systems integrate with most modern CRM/database systems so you don't have to maintain email addresses in your membership director and your email marketing platform. That is a recipe for confusion.

Facebook

Facebook is the largest social media platform and, despite recent concerns about the data safety, Facebook isn't going anywhere. The majority of your congregation probably have Facebook accounts and look at them regularly. That would certainly be true for your community. Facebook allows you to create a page for your church, groups associated with that page, and to run ads directed toward specific audiences. It can be a bit complicated, so working with someone trained in social media tools would save you time and money. Or, you can watch YouTube videos. That is usually my "go to."

Twitter

Twitter is one of the fastest-growing social media platforms. It's ideal for time-sensitive comments, announcements, and updates. Twitter lets you make short posts about anything, but you are limited to only 280 characters in length. Churches use Twitter to send out daily devotions and scripture lessons, highlight memorable lines from the sermon, advertise community events, remind people about church events, and post news alerts from church leaders. You will need to encourage your members to follow your church on Twitter for this to be an effective tool.

Instagram

Instagram is a social networking app made for sharing photos and videos from a smartphone. Churches use Instagram to promote their service times, upcoming events, sermon topics, and devotional messages. You will want to create memes—sharable captioned photos that are designed to be read quickly—that you post on Instagram. For that, I recommend using Canva (http://canva.com/).

Podcasts

Think of a podcast as talk radio on demand. Podcasts form the fastest-growing medium in the marketplace today. Some people have been doing podcasts for a while, and they have a large following. These people are called "influencers" because they can distribute online podcasts to lots of people in a short time with measurable impact. If you have lots of time on your hands and a love for this medium, create your own podcast. Know going in, though, that you have to stick with it over time. It takes a while to build an audience.

You need to know about these tools, but you don't need to be an expert in them. You do need to *find* experts in them. Hire or barter with them. Get them on your team. When you use these tools to their fullest power, you will be amazed by the results.

Marketing Best Practices

If you talk to people working in marketing today, they tell you that it's not possible anymore to over-communicate a message. We used to say that someone had to hear something seven times before they would remember it. Recently, I saw a great description of where we may be today in communication repetition:

1. The first time people look at any given ad, they don't even see it.

2. The second time, they don't notice it.

3. The third time, they are aware that it is there.

4. The fourth time, they have a fleeting sense that they've seen it somewhere before.

5. The fifth time, they actually read the ad.

6. The sixth time, they thumb their nose at it.

7. The seventh time, they start to get a little irritated with it.

8. The eighth time, they start to think, "Here's that confounded ad again."

9. The ninth time, they start to wonder if they're missing out on something.

10. The tenth time, they ask their friends and neighbors if they've tried it.

11. The eleventh time, they start to remember wanting a church exactly like this for a long time.

12. The twelfth time they see the ad, they go to church.

Clearly, repetition matters. What you say, how you say it, and how often you say it is the key to effective communication. In every church I am working with today, I hear the common complaint: "We are terrible at communicating what is going on. I have a hard time keeping it all straight. I can't imagine what new visitors must think."

I don't think we are any better or worse about communicating what is happening at the church than we have been in the past. We have more competition when it comes to getting our message through. With the explosion of new media for communication (social media, email, text messages, websites, podcasts), most churches are ill-prepared to communicate a message twelve times to get someone to church.

Because people now have so many messages hitting us all day every day, designing a communication strategy for your messaging matters. If you don't coordinate your tools and refine your messaging for each environment, you will never be effective. Here is the model that I use:

Marketing Strategy Worksheet						
Publication Date	Message	Publishing Mediums	Target Audience	Title	Call to Action	Notes
June 14, 2018	Community Protest	Facebook, Instagram, Pinterest, Twitter	Members	We March On!	Meet up in Piedmont Park at 8am	We need people to register if possible
June 14, 2018	Community Protest	Website	Members	We March On!	Meet at the park and bring...	Connect website to Eventbrite

June 14, 2018	Community Protest	Bulletin	Members	We March On!	Meet at the park and bring...	Give some background as to why this matters
June 14, 2018	Community Protest	Facebook, Instagram, Pinterest, Twitter	Community Members	Let's March Together	Grace Church invites you to meet in the park	Send to community leaders and ask them to publicize as well
June 14, 2018	Community Protest	Calling Campaign	Community Influencers— people with networks	Let's March Together	Join us in inviting people to march	Develop talking points and organizer packet to send after the call

You can see that we have multiple strategies for the same message because it is targeted to different audiences using different communication tools. For this one event, you could have 30 different communication strategies. When you coordinate them together, you build a synergy that can get your message through.

Most churches do *one* of these. They might post an article on their website. Or, they might put an article in the bulletin for three Sundays. Unless you use *all* of your tools, you won't communicate effectively. Try it the next time you need to get word out about something happening at the church. I bet you will see better results.

What All Good Communicators Do

Ingmar Bergman once said, "Facts go straight to the head. Stories go straight to the heart." Good communicators tell stories. They know that we process in narratives. Think about times you have been immersed in a book or started binge-watching a show on Netflix. The emotional experiences you have in those moments are just as real and powerful as the ones you have in your everyday life. We live in a world of stories.

When you consider what and how you are communicating, stories are your secret weapon. Dr. Clarisa Pinkola-Estes, author of *Women Who Run with the Wolves,* is a Jungian analyst and *cantadora,* a keeper of ancient stories. When you listen to her closely, you hear her weave her own wisdom through the storylines of the ancient myths. Instead of telling you facts about a life lesson, she takes you on a journey as she introduces you to little girls with red shoes, and an evil man with a blue beard, and a crazy old woman who holds the wisdom to save a village. You are drawn into "Story" as it unfolds within you. The stories become a part of you, their wisdom coming to you as you need it—even years after hearing them for the first time.

The wisest people I know use stories to teach, inspire, or provoke the rest of us. They know that stories are what make it through the clutter of our minds. It's no coincidence that Jesus taught in parables. As you think about your own leadership—considering the messages you want to communicate to your church, your community, and to the world—can you tell it to us in a story? Can you help us see it in our mind's eye and feel it in our bones? Can you make us laugh and cry and think and grow?

A Personal Practice

Imagine that you are being interviewed by Anderson Cooper about the local opioid crisis that is impacting teenagers in your community. Create a messaging strategy model for the interview.

A Congregational Practice

Design a communication strategy for an upcoming event at the church. Use the Marketing Strategy Worksheet to organize the details. Then, review it. What did you miss? Is it reasonable? If you do everything you've listed, will it work? Do you need to recruit new resources to help you? Then, try it. Learn, debrief, and try again.

Small Group Discussion Questions

1. Have you had moments when your team was miscommunicating or out of alignment? What did you do to resolve the issues?

2. Do you feel communication within the church is clear and effective? If not, what could you do to work on it?

3. What powerful stories can your church tell that are both inspiring *and* tell the story of who you are as a congregation?

4. Do you feel as if you communicate effectively with the wider community? What else could you do?

---

[1] https://mappingpoliceviolence.org/

Chapter Nine

Mayday Moments

Checklist

- ❏ *PANIC!* But don't let anyone see it
- ❏ Pray
- ❏ Check your airspeed and establish glide slope
- ❏ Look for the best place to land
- ❏ Run your checklists
- ❏ Get the plane on the ground!

> *"A pilot who says he has never been frightened in an airplane is, I'm afraid, lying."*
> —Louise Thaden, American aviation pioneer and the first woman to win the Bendix trophy

The typical invitations that I receive to speak at conferences focus on topics such as "The Future of the Church" and "Trends that Define Us." When I started speaking on these topics years ago, we knew that the Church Universal was changing. We saw that evidenced in the changes in attendance and giving patterns, seminary students entering (or not) the seminary systems, denominational offices undergoing what now feels like permanent restructuring. At that point, though, we couldn't see clearly what all of the changes would mean. We were thinking: "What changes should we be making? What do we want for our future? Is this a blip or a paradigm shift?"

Remember the 2009 US Airways Flight 1539 that crash-landed in the freezing Hudson River in New York with 155 people onboard? The plane's engines were crippled by a double bird strike—almost unheard of—just as they were clearing 2800 feet on their initial climb out of LaGuardia. The plane was piloted by fifty-seven-year-old Captain Chelsey "Sully" Sullenberger, a former military fighter pilot who had flown commercial jets since leaving the Airforce in 1980. He was assisted by First Officer Jeffrey Skiles, who was new to flying the A320, but an experienced pilot with over 15,000 flight hours.

The weather that day was beautiful. They had ten miles visibility with broken clouds at 3700 feet, winds at 8 knots from 290 degrees. Sullenberger even remarked to Skiles, "What a view of the Hudson today." But then the unthinkable happened. Bird strike. Both engines out. Only 2800 feet off the ground and flying at 185 knots groundspeed. With such little altitude, Sullenberger had very few options and no room for mistakes.

As he took manual control of the plane, he radioed a mayday call to the tower at LaGuardia. "Cactus 1549, hit birds, lost thrust in both engines, we are turning back towards LaGuardia." The tower responded, "Okay, you need to turn back to LaGuardia, turn left heading 220." The tower then cleared them to land on Runway 13 at LaGuardia, stopping all other traffic on the runways. Sullenberger called back and said they wouldn't make it. Quickly, they considered the airports in New Jersey. Teterboro airport might be possible. The controller cleared that airport, but after a few minutes Sullenberger came back over the radio and said, "We can't do it... We're gonna be in the Hudson." Ninety seconds later, Flight 1549 made an unpowered ditching at 125 knots into the middle of the Hudson River. And...no one died that day.

In later interviews, Captain Sullenberger stressed that while no pilot ever wants the experience of a double engine failure at only 2800 feet in the air, their relentless training and years of experience ensures that they know how to diagnose the issues and take the necessary action to ensure the safest outcome. But here is the leadership lesson that can get lost: They had to rely on their instincts, experience, and training to safely land that plane. No one had written a checklist for a double engine failure at such a low altitude. They were on their own to decide the next best step.

The Crisis Compass

Knowing when to declare an emergency isn't always obvious. Piloting magazines are filled with stories of pilots who didn't realize the trouble they were in until too late. To help diagnose the situation and determine if we are dealing with a crisis, I use a "Crisis Compass" framework.

Pilots get into trouble for four main reasons:

1. Loss of Control

2. Engine Failure

3. Running Out of Fuel

4. Hazardous Weather

As congregational leaders, we experience these moments as:

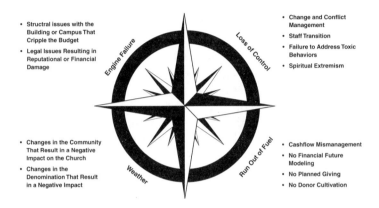

- Structral issues with the Building or Campus That Cripple the Budget
- Legal Issues Resulting in Reputational or Financial Damage

- Change and Conflict Management
- Staff Transition
- Failure to Address Toxic Behaviors
- Spiritual Extremism

- Changes in the Community That Result in a Negative Impact on the Church
- Changes in the Denomination That Result in a Negative Impact

- Cashflow Mismanagement
- No Financial Future Modeling
- No Planned Giving
- No Donor Cultivation

Any one of these four conditions can compromise your congregation; combine them, and you will be in for a terrifying, potentially life-threatening ride.

Hazardous Attitudes

Crisis conditions are usually caused by human error. We fail to act quickly enough. We act too quickly and overcorrect. We ignore the issues. Most accidents in aviation are caused by the story that is going on inside of our heads. We all have thought patterns that guide our most instinctive actions. A big part of aviation training is honing those instincts to consistently deliver the best and safest outcome. For example, let's imagine that we are flying and all of our electronic instruments suddenly fail. We have lost our ability to communicate with air traffic control, our measures of ground speed and fuel burn, our autopilot and our navigation. We are flying thousands of feet in the air without knowing where we are, where we should go, or when we might get there. Yet, even in that situation, we have many options before us. We could:

- Fly the plane straight and level while running through our checklists and watching for a safe place to land (always the best idea)

- Decide that we are going to die, and there is nothing we can do (resignation)

- Decide that we can be heroes and land on a highway or field without running through any of our emergency checklists (machismo)

- Decide that FAA regulations don't apply to this situation and make up our own rules (anti-authority)

- Decide to complete the flight as filed because we are awesome pilots and know that we will be fine (invulnerability)

- Do something, anything, quickly! (impulsivity)

In aviation training, you are taught exactly what to do in these situations...over and over and over. Your instructors do this because they want to be sure that, when you find yourself in a crisis situation, you have the muscle memory to react in the safest and fastest way possible. In this case, after you ran your checklists and determined that your instruments had truly and permanently failed, you would use a technique called deduced reckoning (often also called "dead reckoning") to navigate to an airport or safe place to land. Basically, you look out your window. You look at the sky to spot any stars or the position of the sun, look at the ground, and, if available, use a paper map to determine your best guess location based on outside references that you can see from your plane. Based on that, you can then gain a sense of your direction of flight, your speed, and the wind direction.

Reckon comes from the Old English *recenian,* meaning "to narrate." Deduced narrating. You are literally reimagining the story of how you are getting from Point A to Point B. You are claiming control of how you will lead forward in the crisis. Remember the wise words from Captain Tammie Jo Shults: "As long as you have altitude and ideas, you're okay." Ideation is at the heart of deduced narrating.

Loss of Control

Congregations lose control and stability in four main ways: poor change management, unaddressed conflict, leadership misconduct, and theological laziness or hijacking. Each of these areas is complex, can be interdependent, and will require both training and instincts to navigate gracefully. Most congregations are harmed by the first two more consistently, so let me say a word about these.

Change isn't easy, and while it does occur naturally in many settings, churches tend to consciously or unconsciously put into place systems and structures to resist change. Ironically, their resistance to change can be so great that they are willing to change leaders rather than adapt their structures, policies, or procedures to a healthier adaptation. The myth that keeps most churches on the road to decline is that "healthy churches are free of conflict." That is a lie. *Dying* churches are free of conflict.

John P. Kotter, author of *Leading Change,* says the place to start with healthy change is creating a sense of urgency. He suggests that, in a company with 100 employees, at least a dozen must be motivated to go far beyond their routine efforts if change is to take effect.[1] That number may be slightly higher in congregations. It may be that 25 percent of the membership must get a sense of urgency in a church before change will begin to happen. Creating a sense of urgency may be done in most situations by a frank description of the current situation and the resulting trajectory. You need only run the numbers in most cases.

When I was a denominational executive working in the area of new church development, I ran the numbers on how many churches we were adding and losing in the denomination each week. At one point, we were losing seven churches each week, and starting three new ones. That's not encouraging math. When I started saying that out loud, it got attention. That attention resulted in action. The denomination (for a brief moment) invested significant emphasis and financial resources into starting new congregations. At the end of that time, we were closing three churches per week and starting two. Not perfect, but much better.

Along with a sense of urgency, we also need a clear vision for the future. As I heard Dr. Fred Craddock once say "good preaching is not so much speaking to people as it is speaking for people." By that he meant that good preaching isn't when people are awed by the preacher's wisdom and insight, but when they are allowed to discover their own. In the church a visionary leader is one who helps the people discover the vision for their church that they already treasure in their hearts, and then organizes and articulates that vision back to them.

Communication then becomes key. As the adage goes, "Surprised people behave badly." When change is happening, people are naturally anxious. You literally can't over-communicate in this type of environment. Communication has key benefits[2]:

1. It fills in the voids of unknown information and corrects misinformation;

2. stops rumors;

3. shows that leaders are aware of the changes and are attending to them;

4. reinforces the congregation's vision, mission, and values;

5. strengthens the congregation's sense of community;

6. bolsters morale;

7. empowers people by helping them see the difference they can make;

8. exposes gaps in strategy and implementation.

Communication becomes the oil of your congregational change process; without it, the engine of your change process will grind to a halt.

Finally, you want to develop a bias for action. Change is established when people behave differently. You need to get people busy doing ministry, not management. The late social ecologist and business guru Peter Drucker, who was also a man of faith, said, "The business of the church is to change people; the business of a corporation is to satisfy them."[3] Change is the constant of your congregational life; your role as a leader in the system is to guide people through the process in the same way Jesus did:

- He told them the truth and challenged them to change;

- He taught them and encouraged them;

- He led them into the presence of God;

- He gathered them into community and had them grow together;

- He sent them out to help and heal; and

- He gave them hope of resurrection.

If the church can be the body of Christ in these ways, not only will it be transformed, but it will once more be a transforming power in the world.

Engine Failure

Engine failures have to do with potentially cataclysmic crises that could irrevocably compromise your church. These include major maintenance issues with your building or campus, or legal issues that could result in reputational and financial damage.

St. John's Church had a beautiful 100-year-old oak tree in the center of their children's playground. For years it provided shade to the hundreds of kids who played there between the preschool program and Sunday mornings. Then, the unthinkable happened. The morning of April 17, the wind was blowing strongly, bringing a storm in later than afternoon. The teachers thought the kids would be fine to play for about forty-five minutes until the church service finished. As seven-year-old Zachary was sitting on the seesaw, one of the huge, old oak branches broke off and came down straight onto him. His head was crushed. The teachers rushed over to help, calling 911 on the way. He was taken to the hospital, where he remained in a coma for four weeks until he finally passed away.

Of course, everyone was devastated. Zach's parents filed legal action against the church to help pay the medical bills. The church leaders were quite understanding about this, believing that their insurance policy would kick in and cover this terrible tragedy. But then they got the call that would change everything: they were not covered in this particular case.

The church didn't have endowments or a rainy-day fund. They were vulnerable. After one year of legal negotiations, the church agreed to sell its building and give most of the proceeds to Zach's family. Today, the congregation meets in a rented space in another local church in the area.

This tragic situation represented a total engine failure for St. John's Church. They were able to survive as a congregation, but they suffered major damage in the process. To avoid these kinds of situations, you want to be sure that you have measured the liability you carry on your campus and your buildings. You can never be too prepared.

Run Out of Fuel

I have yet to work with a congregation that has built out financial futuring models based on best guesses for future financial needs. Given that the two largest expenses in every congregation are the building and the staff, you can build any number of models that help you see what results if something happens to either. Instead, church leaders look at their budget vs. actual and balance sheets during their meetings. That's fine, but this practice only shows you what you had in the past and what you have right now. It doesn't help you predict what you can invest in the future or when you might run out of money altogether. To me, that is the more interesting information.

The leaders at Circle of Peace in Chicago needed a new building. They had outgrown their current one, but finding a new space in Chicago was no easy feat. They had three possibilities—all at very different prices and with different levels of renovation needed. They would also have to shape their ministries differently depending on which option they choose, because of the differing physical spaces of each.

The leaders created financial models for each space. They determined the initial purchase and renovation costs for each. That part was easy. But then they needed to dream about the kinds of ministries they could run from those spaces and the staffing they would need. Each model forced them to think carefully through each detail of future costs. With one building, they would be able to offer the most programs in the best location, but would burn through their cash within forty-eight months. The second space needed the most work, and the location would limit their access to the community they wanted to serve, but they could conserve their cash for the longest time. The third space was on the transit line, was the smallest space, and needed some work, but they could partner with some other organizations to offer the programs they wanted in the community. That model had them exhausting their reserves (assuming no additional grants, donations, etc.) in fifteen years. That was their answer! They knew that they had a ten-to-fifteen year runway to make sure they secured additional funding streams, assuming all other assumptions remained the same.

No church should be surprised if it runs out of cash. You should be monitoring your cash flow and anticipating future cash needs every month, if not every week. Capital is the fuel that keeps your church flying.

Weather

Weather is everything that happens outside that you can't control, but can certainly control you. In flying, a pilot's greatest fear is "icing." Ice on your wings is really bad. In the church, events that happen outside of the church's control but that negatively impact the church are the makings of a bad day.

For years now, we have been learning of massive sexual abuse of children by Roman Catholic priests. Every time a new story hits the news cycle, not only are we all heartbroken and horrified, but we are implicated by association. Many people are not sophisticated enough in their understanding of church history to know the difference between the Roman Catholic Church and everyone else. The message they hear is: "Religious leaders molest children." I am convinced that this seemingly endless scandal is doing great harm to all of Christianity. It's like flying straight into a hurricane.

We can also be implicated by events that happen at other famous churches. Willow Creek Church is currently embroiled in a sexual misconduct scandal involving their senior pastor, a man whom millions have followed for years through his sermons and books. He has served in national leadership roles as an advisor to U.S. Presidents, and as a keynote speaker at countless events. This scandal is shocking and terribly sad. Once again, it reinforces the impression that Christianity is corrupt, doing major damage to our "brand."

However, we can also have *wonderful* things happen outside of our control that add a tailwind to our flight. Recently, Episcopal Church Presiding Bishop Michael Curry was invited to preach at Prince Harry and Meghan Merkel's royal wedding. Millions of people around the world watched as the first African American Presiding Bishop gave the sermon of a lifetime. He electrified the attendees and television viewers alike with his call for "Love." People watching who had been estranged from church thought, "Well, if church is like that, count me in!" For two weeks afterward, Episcopal churches saw an increased interest in their churches online, and some churches saw an increase in Sunday attendance.

The key to navigating through weather is to anticipate it before it hits you. You need to be ready for what comes your way. We know we live in an age of increased transparency. We have to be willing to look at our communities with open eyes, even if that means seeing and facing something we'd rather not. When scandal hits, we can't ignore it any more than a pilot can ignore a storm. The first step in navigating safely through bad weather is admitting the weather is there. It's harder to predict the positive waves (unless we intentionally create them). As soon as you see it coming, get ready to ride it out. Get a plan in place, communicate your vision, mobilize your people, and make the best of the ride.

Solving a Problem vs. Treating a Condition

This leads us to talk about problems and conditions. In the Crisis Compass, some of the crises that arise are situational and easy to fix. If the roof leaks, fix it. Others are conditional; we live in a condition of religious leaders getting caught in scandals. These are not so easy to fix.

I was conducting a series of interviews at a larger urban church. The church's membership was stagnant, and they wanted to work on a strategic plan to get them moving forward. In nearly every interview, someone would say, "We need more young people around here. We need to hire a better youth director. I just don't understand why we don't have any high schoolers anymore." They associated their stagnant growth with not having as many teens in the youth program. Their logic: Our church isn't growing. We need to get more high schoolers, and the church will grow again!

If only it were that simple.

To understand the challenge, we need to acknowledge the difference between a problem and a condition. A problem is something that we solve.

Problem: We need to print bulletins for the service on Sunday.

Solution: Print the bulletins.

Problems have solutions. Many times, the solutions are obvious, and we know how to respond. Sometimes, the solutions require some learning before we know the "fix," but once we gain enough information, we can apply a solution that solves the problem.

Conditions are entirely different. We don't solve conditions; we treat them. Conditions are states of being. They speak to the context, the field, in which a problem (or many) might exist. Conditions define the possibilities and limits of the environment in which we are working. When we treat a condition, we are changing the baseline state of being.

Mainline Christianity today exists within the condition of declining attendance at Sunday morning services. We have seen this across the country for some time. People are not going to church as they did in previous generations. That is not likely to change. Declining attendance is a condition of our age. How might we treat that condition? Any number of ways, all of which will have iterative impact.

Condition: Fewer people of all ages are going to church.

Treatments:

> Stop requiring Sunday morning to be the only time someone "counts."
>
> Involve people in ministry in the community—take church to them.
>
> Build friendships with people that establish trust.
>
> Change service times to a more accessible hour.

All of these, one of these, or none of these may impact the condition. Our job in treating the condition is to set up a series of experiments or inquiries to see. Jim Ollhoff and Michael Walcheski, both systems thinkers and authors of the book *Stepping in Wholes: Introduction to Complex Systems,* offer clues to determine whether you are dealing with a problem or working within the context of the symptom of an underlying condition.[4] You are working with a *condition* if:

1. The size of the problem doesn't fit the amount of time and energy you are spending on it. The issue seems smaller than the effort you are putting into addressing it.

2. People have the power to solve the problem but are choosing not to. They would rather spend their time complaining as opposed to fixing the situation.

3. You have tried to solve the problem repeatedly and haven't been successful. You keep trying to resolve the problem, but it changes into a related issue or keeps turning up.

4. An emotional barrier stands in the way to solving the problem. There are some things that people in the organization seem unwilling to address or even talk about.

5. The problem has a pattern and seems to be predictable.

6. The congregation seems to enjoy or receive some pleasure by keeping the issue alive/around. They would rather focus on the "red herring" than the deeper systemic conditions.

7. A congregation seems stressed out and anxious because no one is addressing the deep change needed. People may be afraid to speak their minds about the true nature of their concerns.

8. Just as you "solve" one problem, another one pops up in its place.[5]

If you are working at the condition level, trying to solve problems simply won't work. You will frustrate your leaders and burn through your resources. You're best served by studying the conditions and the symptoms.

A Personal Practice

Think of some of the challenges you've faced in the last year. Using the "clues" listed above, determine whether these challenges were problems or conditions. Do you consider these problems solved or treated? If so, what can you remember from the experience for the next time you face a similar situation? If not, what might you do differently?

A Congregational Practice

Make a list of some of the conditions surrounding your congregation today, both negative and positive. Brainstorm ways you might treat the negative conditions and use the positive conditions to promote growth (change) in your community?

Small Group Discussion Questions

1. What are your "go to" problem-solving strategies? How open is your congregation when it comes to discussing religious scandals in the news?

2. What resources does your church offer to help congregants deal with these scandals?

3. If you had the opportunity to revisit a past problem your church faced and change the way it was handled, what changes would you make?

---

[1] John P. Kotter, *Leading Change* (Boston: Harvard Business Review Press, 2012), 36.

[2] Adapted from Gregory Hunt, *Leading Congregations Through Crisis* (St. Louis: Chalice Press, 2012), 37.

[3] Quoted in C. Kirk Hadaway, *Behold I Do a New Thing: Transforming Communities of Faith* (Cleveland: Pilgrim Press, 2001), 11.

[4] Jim Ollhoff and Michael Walcheski, *Stepping in Wholes: Introduction to Complex Systems* (Eden Prairie, Minn.: Sparrow Media Group, 2002).

[5] Ibid., 60–62.

Chapter Ten

Making a Successful Landing

Checklist

- ❏ Contact your destination airport for runway clearance, weather updates, and altimeter settings
- ❏ Descend to pattern altitude at the field, entering the pattern at a 45-degree angle on the downwind
- ❏ Manage your speed and add your flaps
- ❏ Establish a 3-degree controlled descent on final approach
- ❏ Land on the centerline at the one-thousand–foot markers

> *"Each generation of pilots hopes that they will leave their profession better off than they found it."*
> —*Chesley Sullenberger, Captain of US Airway Flight 1549*

I write this final chapter sitting on a park bench by what *was* the base of the World Trade Center in Manhattan. Tourists from around the world walk by taking pictures of the 9/11 Memorial fountains. They pause in front of the waterfalls, their eyes large as they take in the overwhelming size of the former buildings' foundations. Then I watch as time after time, each person looks down at the railing in front of them and reads the names of the people who died on that devastating day. They read until they can't hold any more names. Then I watch them turn, many with tears in their eyes, and whisper to their loved ones what I imagine are their memories of that day—where they were, what they felt, who they knew. For those of us who saw the terror of those planes flying into the towers in real time, we will never forget.

In a different part of the city, on Broadway, a new musical has opened called *Come From Away*. It's the story of American Airlines Captain Beverly Bass, and her experience of flying a plane full of 158 passengers from Paris, France, to Dallas, Texas, on September 11, 2001. It's worth noting that Captain Bass is famous in her own right for being the third woman hired as a pilot at American Airlines, and the first to make captain—at age thirty-four.

On that day, she had a normal take off and was flying over the middle of the Atlantic Ocean bound for Dallas, Texas, when she heard over the air-to-air radio that a plane had hit the World Trade Towers. She assumed that it was a small plane, which was bad enough, but it wouldn't be a problem for her flight. Then another pilot announced that a second plane hit the Towers, and it was an American 737. At that point, she and her copilot began planning a diversion.

In a matter of minutes, the New York airspace was closed, followed by all U.S. airspace, forcing over 4000 international flights in the air at that moment to find new places to land. Air traffic control told Captain Bass to expect to land in Gander, Canada. When she reviewed the conditions of the runways in Gander on her charts, she knew her Boeing 777 would be the biggest plane those runways could handle...if they were lucky. Doing some quick calculations, she recalls,

> I was overweight with fuel by 7000 pounds. I knew I was going to be overweight for landing in Gander. It's not something that's unacceptable. The airplane can handle it. But if you land overweight, you have to have a major inspection, and I didn't know what the status of the Gander Airport was. I had to decide if I was going to jettison 7000 pounds of fuel out over the Atlantic, or if I was going to land overweight. I opted to jettison the fuel. We went out and did that, and then came in on a 95-mile final approach to Gander. (paraphrase of interview with Bass)[1]

The Gander Airport was built for service during World War II and, afterward, rarely saw major traffic. Then, within a span of less than 12 hours on September 11, 2001, *thirty-eight* international aircraft and almost 7000 people landed in Gander, nearly doubling the size of its population. When it became clear that the "plane people" were going to be stranded for a few days, the community sprang into action. They housed people in their own homes, cooked every meal, turned the local hockey rink into a freezer for food storage, set up additional phone towers so that people could call home, and cared for the 19 animals stranded on the planes for those days. The people of Gander showed extraordinary hospitality on one of the hardest days in our shared history.

Five days later, on September 16, the FAA opened the U.S. airspace and Captain Bass received word that they were cleared to continue to Dallas. However, when they originally arrived in Gander, they were the thirty-sixth plane to land out of thirty-eight, and the only place to park at that point had been the general aviation ramp, used primarily for small planes. Because of the weight of the plane and the heat baking the ramp over the five days they were stranded there, the plane had sunk into the concrete. As the final challenge of this adventure, Captain Bass had to figure out how to push her plane out of these divots without sucking up any cracked concrete or debris into her engines. Carefully, she revved the low-hang engines and prayed that she didn't destroy them with flying debris in the process. With a huge sigh of relief, she got the plane out, and they took off.

Late in the evening on September 16, the 158 passengers of Flight 49 finally made it to Dallas. During the flight, they had collected donations to send back to the people of Gander as a gift of gratitude for their remarkable hospitality. Every year since, those who are able fly back to Gander for a reunion, celebrating the bonds formed in the crucifixion of a national tragedy. The writers of *Come From Away* stress that this is not a story about September 11. It's about September 12. It's about our rising.

What Is All of This Really About?

These two stories remind me that it's out of the crucifying experiences of life that resurrection comes. Always. The natural rhythm of our cruel and beautiful lives is one of life, death, and life again. We can suffer immeasurable loss—then, within minutes, be greeted with deep compassion. I need both of these stories to remind me that life is both brutal and kind.

We are living in a time that, for the mainline church, is brutal. We are watching the deconstruction of systems, ideas, covenants, and congregations that generations before us invested their lives in creating. There is no magical program, brilliant theory, or angel investor that will halt our decline. In our fear, we attack our leaders and criticize our colleagues. I cringe when I watch people in my own denomination assume the worst of our leaders instead of advocating for the best in all of us. We can be immeasurably cruel to one another while we grasp desperately at dwindling resources and plot our own salvation while ignoring our interdependence. The best advice I can offer in this space is to *lean into* the pain. Don't run from it. Don't strategically plan your way out of it. Don't cling or clutch or horde. *Lean in.* Open up. Let it breathe. As you reach the other side, trust that we will all be okay.

We are also living in a time that, for the mainline church, is kind. We are finding our voice, beginning to act in ways more congruent with our souls. I am inspired by movements such as the Poor People's Campaign and Women's March, who rally thousands of people to show up over and over in public, sacrificial ways that inspire in us the dream of a nation concerned about the common good for everyone. When I see leaders such as Rev. Dr. Jacqui Lewis rally her congregation in New York to be a movement of "Revolutionary Love," and the leaders of Faith in Public Life organizing congregations to show up at state representatives' offices to advocate for more just laws, I have hope. We are fierce in our kindness. We are resurrection on the rise.

Yet I still wonder: What is all of this really about? What is *church* really about? I've always understood the church as being a community with a shared story in our scriptures, which binds us together. Church is about weaving relationships together so that life for all of us is more deeply rooted in Love. Today, I would offer that the church also offers a platform to work together to build a world that acts and advocates for the common good of all of us. We are warriors, lovers, peacemakers, protectors, prophets, thinkers, and dreamers who gather together to celebrate our heritage as children of God. At the same time, we are fearlessly willing to stand up and stand in for those our culture might oppress. When we live consciously aware of our power to shape our world for good, we live lives of meaning. We are our own most fully human and fully sacred expressions. We are whole.

The Gift of Descent

Many of you are serving or attending churches that are in decline. Some of your churches won't survive the coming years. You will face tough decisions about closing, merging, or scaling back. Similar to a pilot reaching retirement age, you will fly your final leg and complete your last landing. You should know that you are not alone. This isn't just happening in the church. We are seeing this happening in publishing, higher education, commercial shopping centers, manufacturing...nearly every industry that shapes our American culture is undergoing seismic transformation marking the closings of countless campuses, stores, and factories. The church is no different.

We have an opportunity in this moment of our great transformation. We can approach this time as survivors, desperately clinging to our structures and ways of being. Or, we can see ourselves as pioneers, setting out in the face of the unknown to discover new ways to live faith-filled lives. The inevitable decline of our structures gives us the chance to let go of what might hold us back from that adventure. Nothing today will be the same ten years from now. Why not architect the kind of faith movement we want to see twenty-to-fifty years from now? What do we have to lose?

In my coaching work, I sometimes work with leaders who are scared of their futures. They can't see through their fear to see their own possibilities. When we get to this point, I have them do a simple exercise:

Find three or four people in your lives who know you well and who care about you. Ask them to get together in person if possible, or on the phone/web-conference if not. Ask them for one hour. When you meet, tell them what you are feeling. Talk about your fears, your anxiety, your hopes...all of the stuff that is swirling around in you that is making it hard to see your next steps. Then ask them, "Based on what I've said, what do you see? What did you hear? What ideas or advice do you have?"

Suffering often comes to us because we are simply out of ideas. Talking to people we trust gives us new insights and perspectives. We borrow their vision until we can see clearly once again on our own.

Congregations can get stuck in fear and anxiety as well. In such a case, talk to others outside of the church to get ideas. Listen to their perspectives. Then, move in the direction that feels most life-giving. Some ideas are restricting and feel small. Those are ones that are the most predicable and usually demand the least courage. Go with the ones that make your eyes light up and make you sit up a bit taller. Follow your gut and choose the future that demands you be both brave and kind.

Learning to Land

As with learning to live a meaning-filled life, learning to land a plane takes practice. In your training, you practice landing hundreds of times. Your first landing is always rough. Your second one, you pancake on the runway and nearly blow out your tires. Your third one, you flare up and bounce back down. Your fourth one, you come in too high. Your fifth one, you come in too fast. Your sixth one, you almost veer off the side of the runway. Your seventh one, you land on your nose wheel... You get the point. You keep practicing until, finally, you start to *feel* the plane. Your body begins to sense the best descent speeds. Your eyes learn how to gage your rate of descent. You can sense your distance from the runway. You trust your instruments, but your body knows too. The best pilots draw on both ways of knowing.

When I get in my plane to take off, I always joke with the ramp attendants that my goal is to bring it back in one piece. When I get out of the plane at the end of the flight, I smile and say "Great news! We can fly the plane again." I hope I am able to say that after every one of my flights. As one pilot recently told me, "Only the take-off is optional." Learning to land a plane requires you commit to three practices:

1. You learn to manage your speed, rate of descent, and flare;

2. You debrief your flight at the end and learn the lessons it offers you;

3. You get ready to go up again.

A successful landing is one sign of a committed pilot. The fact that you don't bounce down the runway or veer dangerously off the side and into the grass is because a good pilot has spent years learning—not just how to land, but how to do everything that leads up to that point. It takes a willingness to learn from each experience and then welcome the next flight for the new adventure that it offers you.

In our congregations, a "successful landing" looks like a community that has learned to trust its deepest instincts and to adapt to its external environment. A successful congregation knows that, just as a pilot has to practice landing hundreds of times before he perfects it, congregation members have to practice living in brave and kind ways over and over before they truly embody a way of being in the world that looks like Jesus'. We try, we fail, we try again. Life, death, life.

Every pilot will also tell you that you need guides along the ways—instructors—who make sure that you aren't learning the wrong techniques or practicing patterns you will have to unlearn later. When you are in a stressful situation, such as landing in low-visibility conditions or with high winds, you want to be sure your training has prepared you. Successful landings are all the more meaningful when they are made in less than ideal conditions.

Landing in Hazardous Conditions

Recent cultural events are analogous to dangerous wind gusts smashing into many of our institutions, denominations, communities, local churches, and possibly even our democracy. We were in a stable, controlled descent on a normal everyday flight—and then, suddenly, we were knocked off course by deep theological divisions that ultimately have political implications. Every landing requires a unique strategy. I am watching all of us wrestle to find the best approach.

The trouble is that I see examples of every kind of hazardous attitude. I see churches and pastors pretending that nothing has changed (invulnerability); I see church leaders locally and nationally rallying people for petitions and protests, without any larger strategy behind them (impulsivity); I see church members threatening to leave their denominations because they can't see what those denominations bring to the crisis at hand (anti-authority); I see brazen church leaders proclaiming that *they alone* have the solutions to our impotence and decline (machismo); I see too many church leaders trying to simply hold on until they retire in the next few years and can hand this mess over to someone else (resignation).

Our job is to trust our best instincts and to adapt to our unexpected environment. Our training has taught us to land in conditions in which people treat one another with genuine respect, religious leadership has an air of respectability within our communities, and the "brand" of Christianity isn't a label that makes us squirm. But on our *current* flight, we find ourselves landing in an unexpected environment—one ripe with rampant racism, corruption, conflict, and social instability—forcing us to draw on a deep reserve of training, practice, and wisdom. This landing is not like what we have practiced in the past.

We need to decide on our landing strategy. We have the opportunity in this moment to change the story that we are telling about Christianity in this country. We can adopt a landing strategy of defeat. We can talk about the day the evil empire of the Alt-Right and the Religious Right took over Christianity and corrupted our nation. We can tell a story about how the decline of our congregations was just too great, that our denominations and seminaries didn't equip us to lead in this time. We can tell the story about a generation of donors dying off and our churches just not being able to sustain their budgets.

Or, we *could* design a strategy based in courage. We could tell a story of how we rallied our communities, networked our congregations, launched a coordinated national media strategy, built new partnerships with the private sector, cultivated a new funding base, influenced major legislation, hosted national events, and generated mobile apps, books, podcasts, sermons, songs, courses, studies, and software—all of which reclaimed a just and generous Christianity and changed the course of human history.

That is the strategy that honors our calling. Ours is a story of *HOPE*. We were made for this moment. The Church was made to lead in this time, and you are called to embody that leadership. Of this I am certain. Should we fail to rise to this opportunity, we will doom ourselves to irrelevance and continue on our path of decline. Romans 5:4–5 reminds us:

> There's more to come: We continue to shout our praise even when we're hemmed in with troubles, because we know how troubles can develop passionate patience in us, and how that patience in turn forges the tempered steel of virtue, keeping us alert for whatever God will do next. In alert expectancy such as this, we're never left feeling shortchanged. Quite the contrary—we can't round up enough containers to hold everything God generously pours into our lives through the Holy Spirit! *(Message)*

I believe this to be true. My life to this point has proven it so. I suspect yours has as well. The question now is: Where to start?

Our Next Flight

I am convinced that a new kind of Christianity—and a new kind of church as its earthly expression—is emerging in our midst. This new Christianity relies far less on structure and institution; it is a raw spiritual expression of a living, boundless God. This new Christianity is a faith on the move, moving from being an organized religion to an organizing religion. This new Christianity is kind, generous, brave, and always on the side of the oppressed. It's not theologically agnostic or vague about what it stands for. It supports women's rights and LGBTQ rights, welcomes immigrants, values collaboration, seeks love in all its forms, and is reclaiming the ancient spiritual practices that help our souls deepen.

I am also convinced that this new kind of Christianity is at a tipping point. We face the reality that it will either be a growing movement that reclaims an ancient faith for the common good of all, or it will become a fringe movement with two distinct factions: the progressives who don't matter at all, and the extremists who terrorize us all. The choice is ours.

See you in the skies, friends. It's time to take flight.

A Personal Practice

Think of three of the most creative, courageous people you know. On a piece of paper, tell each of their life stories to this date (researching as necessary). What was their life like as a child? What experiences helped them tap into their creativity? What experiences hurt them? Where do you think they found their sources of inspiration? At what point did they break out of the predicted pattern and do something noteworthy or courageous?

After you have written the stories of these people you admire, write your own story down. Do you see the similarities? Do you feel empowered in ways you hadn't before? Sometimes we admire people who are a lot like ourselves.

A Congregational Practice

Think about your denomination's history—times when it stood up as one united voice to take a stand that you now view as being on the right side of history. What do you think it cost the leaders at that time? What do you think they gained? What evidence can you see that their courage made a difference?

Small Group Discussion Questions

1. Do the members of your congregation hold the same opinions about the challenges facing Christianity today? If not, how can you address these differing opinions in a constructive manner?

2. Does your congregation have an environment in which people feel comfortable discussing differing opinions? If so, how can you ensure that environment lasts? If not, how can you create one?

3. Why are you hopeful about the future of church?

---

[1] Interview of Captain Beverly Bass; found at https://www.youtube.com/watch?v=6oxRnWeXnm8